IN THE LIMELIGHT

IN THE

HARPER
An Imprint of HarperCollins*Publishers*

Why Don't We: In the Limelight
Copyright © 2018 by Signature Entertainment, LLC
Photographs on pages 4, 6, 7, 13, 24, 42, 58, 60, 76, 99, 100, 101, 103, 104, and 195 provided by authors.
All photographs copyright © 2018 by Signature Entertainment, LLC
Photographs by Zack Caspary. Additional photos provided by Mike Lerner and August Reinhardt.

For information address HarperCollins Children's Books, a division of HarperCollins Publishers, 195 Broadway, New York, NY 10007.
www.harpercollinschildrens.com

Library of Congress Control Number: 2018952013
ISBN 978-0-06-287131-2

Typography by Lissi Erwin/SplendidCorp.
18 19 20   CG/WOR   10 9 8 7 6 5
❖
First Edition

LIMELIGHT

WHY DON'T WE

CONTENTS

Letter to Our Fans

We've come so far in the past two years. We've worked super hard along the way, but you guys are the ones who made all of this happen. Everyone who watched our videos online when we were just starting out, everyone who supported us on our early tours, everyone who learns the lyrics to our songs or comes to our shows—we couldn't do this without you. We're the luckiest guys ever, and we're so excited for everything that comes next. With you guys at our side, we know it'll be dope.

♥**Love,**
Corbyn, Daniel, Zach, Jonah,
and **Jack**

TO: *You*

FROM: WHY DON'T WE

PART I

MADE
FOR
IT

CHAPTER 1

THE BRAINIAC
Corbyn

"Corbyn is like a cool, geeky nerd. He's really smart. He knows who he is."
—Daniel

I've always been super driven. When I was two, my mom says I refused to take naps. "Then I'll miss out on everything!" I cried. I had FOMO before FOMO was even a thing!

From the get-go, I had this crazy curiosity about the world and I was lucky that my mom allowed and encouraged me to be really independent. She definitely wasn't one of those helicopter parents, hovering over my brother and sister and me every second of the day. She let us learn on our own and I was like a sponge, soaking up everything. She gave me my first book in kindergarten, and it was about space. I taught myself to read it in one day. Later, I asked her, "Did you know astronauts experience weightlessness?" She freaked out that I even knew how to pronounce such a big word. She let us explore outside, too. From a very young age, I was allowed to ride my bike around the neighborhood

alone. I climbed on roofs, rode dirt bikes, and crawled in the sewers. Not in poo, like when the sewer was dry! (Though occasionally there were some weird substances . . .)

I was a little reckless, but I knew my rights from my wrongs, so I stayed out of trouble for the most part. That helped my mom trust letting me do stuff. She was always there for us whenever we needed her, but she really let us push our limits and boundaries and I'm grateful for that.

My dad was more the disciplinarian type. He was a military guy, in the air force, and flew F-15 Eagles and B-1 bombers before he retired as a lieutenant colonel. My dad has crazy stories he's promised he'll tell me one day, as long as they're not classified! He's a very smart man and I have great admiration for him.

Because my dad was in the military, we moved around all the time when I was young. I was born in Texas, but he was stationed in Florida, South Dakota, and Alabama before we put down roots in Virginia. Sometimes being an army brat is hard on a kid and makes you shy or a loner or scared of change. But I was the exact opposite. I adapted to new situations quickly and learned to make new friends easily. I definitely was sad whenever we left for the next base but I had the attention span of a goldfish, so it took, like, a week, and then I was over it!

It was way harder saying goodbye to my dad when he was deployed: that dreaded day when my family drove to the base and watched my dad step on the plane, never sure when (or if) he'd come back. I never knew exactly where he was. We could Skype sometimes but, back then, Skype was sketchy. The longest I didn't talk to him was six months. That was rough on all of us, especially my mom.

Since my dad was gone most of the time, my mom was my rock. She was the person I could always go to, to trust that I was safe and okay. Looking back, I was treated as the man of the house. I was young, so I couldn't take on that much responsibility, but my mom conditioned me in that way—you know, "You're the oldest. This is the time to step up and grow up and learn about life."

Kudos to her for that because it helped me become as independent as I am today.

I taught myself everything—reading, art, and, of course, music. It was always a huge part of my life. When I was a toddler, I belted out Michael Jackson and Backstreet Boys in my booster seat in the car. My dad might not have physically been around, but his influence on me was strong. He was from New Orleans and loved listening to jazz and the blues. But my mom was my biggest influence. She played piano and the harp. She'd play "Colors of the Wind" from *Pocahontas*, although I admit I didn't appreciate it back then. She gave me my first mini keyboard in kindergarten and claims I taught myself how to play it by ear by the time she cooked dinner.

The funny thing is that, as I got older, music was not my main focus. I liked sports, and I was a pretty decent football player, but I was a skinny kid. I played four seasons of tackle, but I was getting pummeled so I gave it up. Back then, my burning passions were video games, art, and graphic design. We didn't have a lot of money, so my entrepreneurial spirit kicked in early. The first money I ever made was selling kids personalized screen savers for a dollar. I got obsessed with video editing, too. When I was a freshman in high school, I took clips of video game kill feeds, synced the gunshots to music, and designed crazy effects. I could happily spend seven hours a day after school in my basement editing just one fifteen-second clip. It had to be perfect. I had a lot of determination!

I really thought I'd ultimately have a career in video game editing. Either that or something science-y like engineering, since I was taking honors, AP, and college-level classes and had a 4.1 GPA. My whole life had been leading up to me getting a scholarship to a good school, like Cornell or maybe even MIT.

Singing wasn't in the master plan.

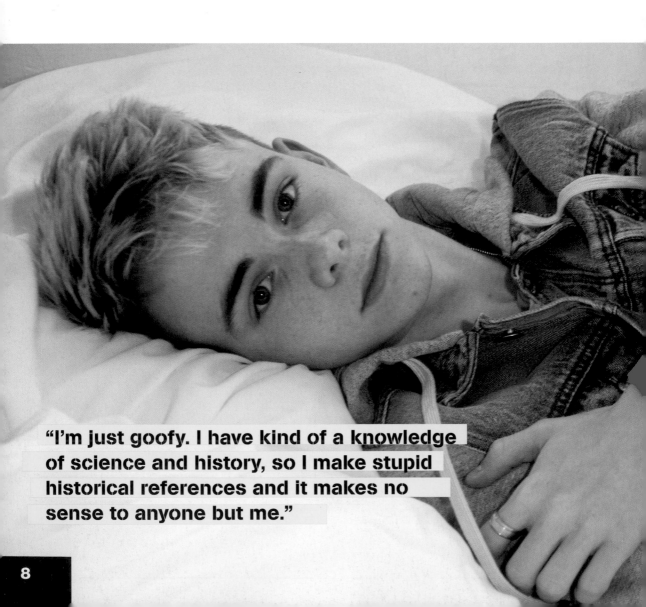

"I'm just goofy. I have kind of a knowledge of science and history, so I make stupid historical references and it makes no sense to anyone but me."

There's a saying, "Life is what happens while we are making other plans"—and that makes a lot of sense to me. A series of unexpected events took me on a path I never could have seen coming.

When I was twelve, my mom surprised me with my first real electric guitar, after she saw me slay an Aerosmith song on *Guitar Hero*. I went back to the basement and taught myself chords from YouTube tutorials and before I knew it I was shredding Three Days Grace and Five Finger Death Punch.

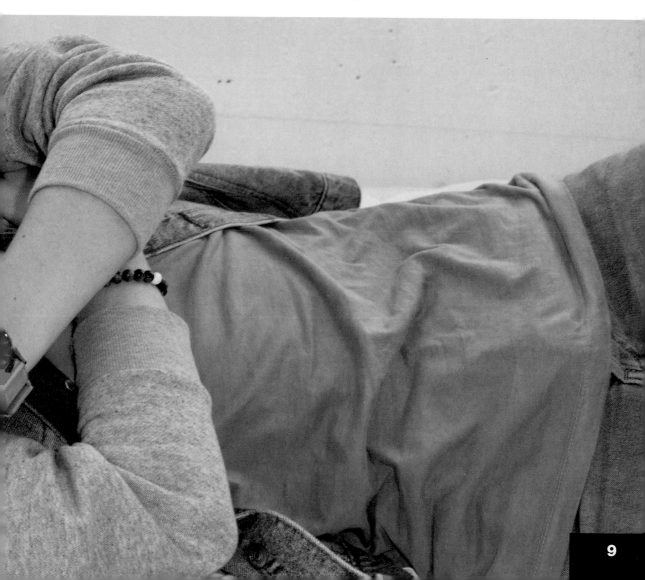

Next, I branched out to mellower, folky genres. I stole my dad's crappy sixteen-year-old acoustic guitar and played Taylor Swift songs and "Collide" by Howie Day. I'd never sung for real before, so I hummed along. I don't remember if there was a specific moment that was like, Wow, I can really sing! I'd been belting out music since my booster seat days and I guess I got better with age.

I had a lot of faceless online friends in my Xbox gaming universe and the voice chat was the perfect place to test out my voice on a live audience. I sang Bruno Mars's "Grenade" and "Just the Way You Are." I didn't even know what these people looked like and that made me feel safe. I didn't tell anyone in my real life about it, not even my brother and sister.

Once I got some positive feedback, which boosted my confidence, I posted fifteen-second clips of covers, like "Boomerang" by the Summer Set and "Jumper" by Third Eye Blind, on Instagram. For the first time, my friends at school saw me singing and they loved it. A classmate told me I should check out YouNow, a live video streaming site. "Oh, that sounds fun," I thought. "I'm a weirdo, I'll try it!"

For the next two years, I did live "shows" every day under the musician tab, singing songs and taking requests. I couldn't wait to run home from school and get on the stream. It was hard work, coming up with new material and keeping an audience entertained. I pretty much sang the same songs over and over! But I grew a following and made real cash in my tip jar. Fans could buy gold bar "currency" on the app (which is how the app made money) and leave gold bar tips for singers they liked. Sometimes I made eight hundred dollars per broadcast. The most I ever made was $1,300 in an hour! It was how I built my foundation and brand. I'm pretty sure young girls used their parents' credit cards, so I'm sorry, moms and dads out there!

I set up a budget for myself and bought three things with the money I earned:

1. **Chick-fil-A (eight-piece nuggets, or if I was feeling macho, a twelve-piece, and a large fries)**
2. **Taco Bell (chicken quesadillas ONLY because they are so dank in the good way!)**
3. **An iPad Mini with a stand**

Besides wasting my money on junk food, I invested in equipment for my broadcast. Now I could see more comments on my live feed and interact with my

"Corbyn can do really cool, quivery things with his voice."
—Jonah

new fans on my phone and iPad at the same time. Eventually I bought a webcam and a new computer with my tips. I had more control over how the video looked: the contrast and the colors.

My parents, who were amicably separated by this time, supported and nurtured my new hobby. When my dad was home, he invited me to visit him at his new home in Williamsburg, Virginia. He told me to bring my guitar but didn't say why. Then he took me to an open mic karaoke contest at a coffee shop. "You're singing tonight," he said with a sneaky grin. I was so nervous performing in front of less than twenty people, because I could see their reactions. But he had bigger plans for me. He knew I needed much more experience live, on a stage.

My dreams of being a video editor or an astronaut for NASA were out the window. I bought the domain for CorbynBesson.com myself and made a logo for my custom merchandise—shirts, hoodies, posters, and bracelets. I processed all the orders, wrote up the labels, and shipped out all the merch at the post office. It was my own little business.

Sophomore year, I got signed to go on the Impact tour with other social media stars. That's when I met two insanely amazing singers named Jack Avery and Zach Herron. I did another conference called Magcon, where I hung out with a handsome, talented fella named Jonah Marais. And I was emailing with a cool young dude named Daniel Seavey, who I befriended after watching him kill

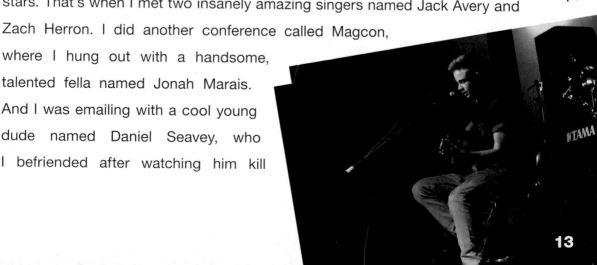

Leonard Cohen's "Hallelujah" on *American Idol.*

I was on the road for the next year. I missed a lot of school. My teachers didn't really know what was going on. I should have been taking multivariable calculus (I don't know what that means, either) and applying to colleges.

Instead, I decided to join a band with some random guys I met on those tours.

Was it reckless? I don't think so. I'd call it a leap of faith!

"Corbyn sees the best in everyone and really makes an effort to keep everyone around him in a positive mind-set."
–Daniel

WHY ... I WANT TO BE A STYLE ICON

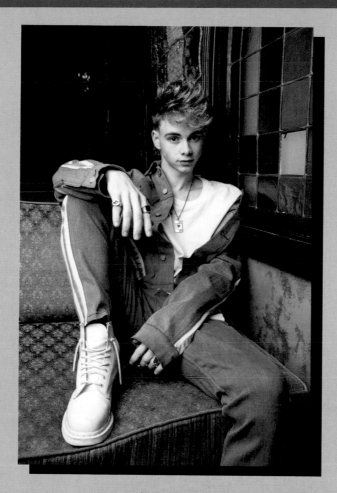

I've never been afraid to express myself, and my style is a very important part of my creative process. One day I hope to have my own clothing line!

CLOTHES

When I was younger, I only wore PacSun, Zumiez, and loose-fitting joggers with, like, a maroon shirt. Now I'm really into streetwear.

SHOES

I'm a shoe fanatic. The craziest pair of shoes I ever bought were my first Yeezys. I also like Adidas NMD and Dr. Martens boots. I have a white leather pair of the boots—that's such a standout look, when the white is so big on your foot. It adds a cool grunge look.

FRAGRANCE

I have three different ones. They all invoke different moods:

Versace Eros—When I smell it, I think of the color teal. It's got a cleaner, sexy smell. It says "young bad boy"!

Yves Saint Laurent L'Homme—It's a little classier, not as strong, a mature kind of scent. This is what I was wearing when I met Taylor Swift!

BVLGARI—is a mix of both scents, the classy bad boy.

HAIR

I bleach it. That's my thing now. I did it to do something different and it stuck and now I like it.

WHO, WHAT, WHEN, WHERE, WHY

MY MOTTO:

"Do you." Two simple words. What you like is what you like. No one should dictate what you should properly like or properly say or wear.

FAVE FOOD:

Penne alla vodka

CHILDHOOD NICKNAME:

Corby Worby

LEAST FAVE FOOD:

I'm not really a sandwich guy. I would never eat my sandwiches that my mom would pack me. Turkey and cheese on wheat bread? Get it away! I also

hate squash and mushrooms. The texture and the sliminess just kills me. Ugh!

FAVE BINGE:

The Walking Dead and *Stranger Things*. And I love *Rick and Morty*—it's the kind of show where I can collect my weird thoughts and watch them happen on the screen.

PERSONAL THEME SONG:

"Cotton-Eye Joe"

SPECIAL TALENT:

I'm really good at remembering Wi-Fi passwords and phone numbers.

HOW I DE-STRESS:

I started listening to Frank Ocean at a really good time in my life. I was back home and felt really happy about my friends and about myself.

FAVE APP:

VSCO

FAVE VIDEO GAME:

PUBG

FAVE HOLIDAY:

Thanksgiving because my birthday is right around Thanksgiving. Sometimes it lands ON Thanksgiving! I'll have cake and then we'll do turkey at night. Heyyyyy!

BROKEN BONE:

I fractured my pinkie in sixth grade playing kickball and had to have a cast for four weeks. They gave me a pink cast for some reason and all my friends signed it and it made it funny!

"Corbyn gives me facts when I need it."
—Zach

19

DREAM VACATION:

I've never been on a family vacation. I went on a camping trip for a few days but never a cruise or an exotic island out of the country. I have a secret plan to take my family on a REAL expensive vacation! Errr, maybe not so secret now!

BIGGEST SPLURGE:

My mom's one wish in life is to have a little quaint house on the beach. One day I want to get her a house up in Malibu where she can play her harp.

IF I WASN'T A SINGER, I'D BE…:

An astronaut or a rocket engineer for NASA. I'm so fascinated with outer space.

IF I WAS PRESIDENT:

I would make homework optional!

FAVE ANIMAL:

Definitely a cheetah. They're elegant and quick and just look so dope.

FAVE CEREAL:

Rice Krispies with dribbled sugar on top. If you eat it plain, it's basically just crunching on cornstarch.

MOST TREASURED POSSESSION:

My Louis Vuitton backpack that I bought in Vegas.

DREAM CAR:

A brand-new McLaren or Porsche 911 GT3.

WHAT I LEAST LIKE ABOUT MY APPEARANCE:

I'm really skinny. My body thankfully fits clothing pretty well so I'm like, *Cool, cool*, but under the clothes I'm like, *Ahh, I want to be more built! I need to go to the gym!!*

HIDDEN TALENT:

I'm great at Photoshop and compositing.

BEST PRANK:

For Christmas last year, for no reason, I sent all the guys eggplants. I mailed them anonymously to their parents' houses, addressed to their first and middle names, and included a one-line message: "Sky's so clear when you're the view," a lyric from "Taking You." They didn't think it was funny. They were all really creeped out and thought they had stalkers!

BIGGEST FEAR:

Death! Just cuz I like living. I only get one of these lives and I would hate for it to end short. I just don't want to die. Or centipedes. That thing should not have that many legs!

CHAPTER 2

THE FREE SPIRIT
Jack

**"Jack is hilarious. You can never predict the next words he'll say. It's impossible!"
—Zach**

I grew up in a house full of women. When I was only one year old, my parents split up and my older sister, Sydney, and I lived with my mom. She remarried and had my two little sisters, Ava and Isla . . . so I basically grew up with a bunch of women. There were so many amazing things I learned living with a lot of smart, strong ladies, but one of the biggest lessons was patience! I can't tell you how many times I had to wait for the bathroom or sit in the car alone while they all took forever to get ready and get out the front door. You can't fight it; you just have to accept it and deal.

I'm really grateful that patience was ingrained in me. Otherwise, I might have gone crazy being stuck in my small town. For as long as I can remember, I couldn't wait to get out of Susquehanna, Pennsylvania, population 1,600. Even my mom was always like, "We're gonna get out of this small town someday. It's going to happen."

I'm not trying to knock my hometown. All my best friends from childhood—all the way back to kindergarten—are still my best friends. I graduated with fifty-four kids in my class. I love that in a small town everybody knows everybody. But it just wasn't the right place for me. Small-town people can be small-minded, and I got picked on a lot for being different.

It all started in fifth grade, when my older sister, Sydney, got me into fashion. It wasn't in style back then for guys to have skinny jeans but I wanted them so badly. I couldn't find any, so I started wearing girls' skinny jeans because I wanted mine to be super tight. Welding is big in my town, so everyone else wore big boots and dirty pants. I looked like an LA kid, in painted-on jeans and long shirts. I thought it was dope but everyone was like, "Yo, you're wearing a dress!" I got called "fag" a bunch. Sometimes I got really mad about it, and I'd yell back, "At least I don't wear five-pound boots every day!" But mostly I just ignored it.

Sydney was a huge influence on me. She taught me to be confident in my individuality. She helped me see that you don't always have to follow the crowd; you can do your own thing. We have a favorite song. It's called "Simplethings" by Miguel and it goes:

> **I said, no, I don't need a model**
>
> **Baby, I don't need a debutante**
>
> **Just be a tough act to follow**
>
> **You know, a free spirit, with a wild heart**

I love these lyrics because I've always felt like a free spirit, and the song always reminds me to be myself. "Never be small-minded," my mom always told me. "Always be willing to explore and experience new things."

I had such a hard time sitting still in school, so I hated it. I never got diagnosed with ADHD, but I always needed to move around so much or I felt like I'd jump out of my skin. I wanted to be out in the world traveling and experiencing life. I knew pretty early that music was my ticket out of Susquehanna. I think God does bless people, and I think he blessed me and I thank Him every day for it. Music was also in my genes. My dad is a talented pianist. Every summer, Syd and I visited him in Seattle and he played all this crazy classical music, while we sat at the edge of the piano watching him in awe. Inspired by my dad, I started piano lessons and got pretty good, too.

There was always a lot of music floating around in my house. My mom played a lot of classic stuff like the Beatles and Michael Jackson and, like a lot of boys my age at the time, I worshipped Justin Bieber and Ed Sheeran. I also remember we'd go snowboarding at a ski resort in the winter and in the car on the way there I'd always sing "I'm Yours" by Jason Mraz. When I was about twelve, my mom heard me singing in the shower. She pressed her ear up against the locked bathroom door to be able to get a better listen. Before I went to bed, she asked me to come in her room. She told me she was impressed with my voice and asked me to sing a song for her. So I did Michael Bublé's "Feeling Good." I could tell by her reaction that she was impressed. She encouraged me to keep practicing.

In sixth grade, I taught myself guitar by watching online videos of beginner chords. I couldn't wait to get home every day after school to practice. That was just as fun to me as playing basketball or skateboarding. One summer, when I was fourteen, I went to Nashville to visit my grandparents. I always had a strong spiritual connection to Nashville, aka Music City. All the greatest country artists in history have lived and recorded there. The place has live music pumping just about everywhere, even in little stores that sell cowboy boots! I'd gotten pretty good at my guitar, so I asked my mom if I could go downtown to busk on Broadway and she let me.

The very first time I played in front of people I sang "Banana Pancakes" by Jack Johnson. Within an hour, I had twenty dollars in my pocket! This kid was like, "Hey, man, you're really good. Can I get a picture with you?"

"You want a picture with me?" My sister Sydney and I looked at each other like it was the craziest thing we'd ever heard. "Okay, sure!"

That was the first time I had my picture taken with anyone, and he even posted it on Instagram with the comment, "Check this kid out!" Right there—that's when I knew this was everything I wanted to do. Ever since that moment, I've worked harder and harder to reach my goal.

(Btw, after I made that twenty bucks, I treated my sister to lunch at Panera!)

Once I knew my purpose in life, I put 1,000 percent of my energy into it. I quit the basketball team, even though it was my favorite sport and it killed me. I had

to be realistic—I was a baller, but no way was a five-foot-seven kid going to the NBA! I posted YouTube covers, made my own beats, tried to produce and get my name out there. With my mom's blessing, I skipped taking the SAT and put college on the back burner.

My mom was my biggest champion. She called everyone. She saw my potential and pushed me. She'd be like, "Jack you should get a YouTube video out. Jack you should do this." She set up performances at malls and sent emails on her lunch breaks to anyone she could find who was linked to the music industry. "Someday, someone will see this," she told me, "and it will open a door." She was right. It did.

"If you have a dream you want to achieve, go for that over everything. If you work hard for that, you will get it."

"This path was crazy. It was fate.
It was like, What is happening?"

Once I booked my first social media tour, everything happened so fast. I met Jonah at a show in LA and Daniel on a project we did together in New York. This was when Daniel was small—he eventually hit a crazy puberty growth spurt. But when I met him, he was a little dude shredding on the guitar. I was like, "Wow!"

I got booked on social media tours, like Brave Fest, run by a great guy named Jon Lucero, and Impact, where I met Corbyn for the first time. Corbyn and I had a lot in common, so we became really good friends and vibed out. Zach hopped on the tour for his first show when we hit Indianapolis. We were shocked when more than six hundred people bought tickets to see us. "Holy crap, this is really big," Zach said. I remember to this day, this little man was just fifteen years old and already had 145,000 followers on Instagram. I only had 40,000. He killed his very first performance, and I thought, "Shoot, Zach is just super talented. Maybe the most talented I've ever seen."

Once I started traveling on the social media tours, I never looked back. I was like a caged animal set free. Zach, Corbyn, and I had an insane time touring the country together. We stayed up until 5:00 a.m. making horror stories on Snapchat. Sometimes we'd get so delirious we'd do dumb things like see who could get his face closest to the blades of a moving fan without getting his head chopped off.

It was such good times, but the crazy thing was, none of us had any idea the best was yet to come!

"Always be happy and nice to others. That makes other people happy and that makes everyone happy in general."

WHEN...I TRIED OUT FOR
AMERICAN IDOL

I tried out for *American Idol* the same year Daniel made it. The fans think there's a huge secret about it, so I'm gonna set the record straight. My audition was in a huge gym and I only got thirty seconds to sing for random judges. I was super nervous. I had my guitar and I sang "Too Close" by Alex Clare. After my audition, they said, "That was a great job. I don't think you're what we need for this season. Keep working on it." I was crushed at the time, but looking back, I see why I didn't make it. I went flat and sharp. I didn't know how to smoothly play a rhythm on my guitar while singing at the same time. I needed more practice. Fans think it's a jealousy issue between Daniel and me, and send messages like, "Sorry, Jack. Hope you're okay." Just want everyone to know...I'm fine! I'm in a band!

The Free Spirit—Jack / in the limelight

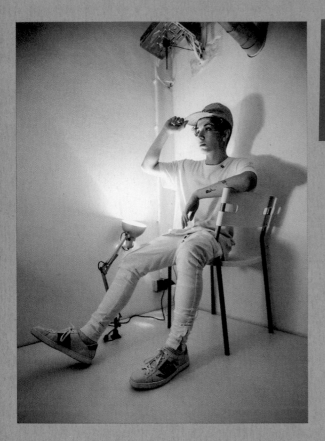

WHO, WHAT, WHEN, WHERE, WHY

MY MOTTO:

"Work until you no longer have to introduce yourself." People might take that as cocky, but in my opinion, it's really cool to have a goal where all the hard work you've done pays off and everyone knows it.

CHILDHOOD NICKNAME:

Little Bubby, Jacko, or Jacky

FAVE BINGE:

Breaking Bad? Honestly I don't remember the last time I watched TV.

FAVE FOOD:

A nice plain cheese pizza with some garlic sauce. I'm a very bland eater. If you give me squid, I'm not trying that.

FAVE APP:

Instagram. I love posting on my feed. I like being artsy and creative and posting stupid videos of Zach and me jamming.

FAVE EMOJI:

The laughing emoji! I'm always laughing when I text people!

CELEB CRUSH:

Selena Gomez

FAVORITE TATTOO:

I have a whole solar system on my arm. It means, no matter what planet you're from, everyone is equal. Another one is a rose for my little sister Isla. She's nine and Rose is her middle name. We have a special bond. We've always been really close. I love kissing her cheeks all the time. She is a little angel!

BEST HIGH SCHOOL MUSICAL MOMENT:

I played Tevye in *Fiddler on the Roof*.

HIDDEN TALENT:

Beatboxing. When I was nine, I made a video to try to get on the *Ellen* show.

DREAM COLLABORATION:

Jaden Smith

FAVE CEREAL:

Cap'n Crunch

BIGGEST FEAR:

Spiders, for sure!

MOST TREASURED POSSESSION:

My mom recently got me a cross necklace and it says, "St. Christopher guide me in all directions." It's for safe travels when I tour.

BIGGEST SPLURGE:

I sent my sister Ava on a trip to Italy and I bought my sister Sydney tickets to Harry Styles's concert. I also surprised my sister Isla on Christmas day with a trip to Disney World. We left that day after she opened the surprise. It was Isla, my mom, and me. So fun!

BEST ADVICE I EVER GOT:

My uncle is a successful entrepreneur and he taught me how to make a vision board. Every new year, you write down your goals, big and small. Hang it somewhere you'll see it every day. The first time I tried it, I wrote getting 50,000 followers on Instagram, meeting cool new people, buying my first guitar, and living life to the fullest. Without realizing it, I crossed off every goal I had for that year!

IF I WASN'T A SINGER, I'D BE:

A professional skateboarder. I've been skateboarding since I was eight. Skateboarding is a huge stress reliever. It makes me happy.

CHAPTER 3

THE BRAVE ONE
Zach

"Zach is fearless. He's not going to let anyone tell him he can't do something."
—Corbyn

I've always been known as "The Singing Kid."

Maybe it's because when I was a baby, my mom and dad sang at least ten songs to me every night before putting me to bed and music infused into my soul. In preschool, I put on a performance for all my teachers almost every single morning. Anytime my parents had company over, I sang for them, did magic tricks, played the drums, and made puppet shows out of Popsicle sticks. I had screenings of little movies I directed, starring my little brother and me. Everyone knew back then I'd be an entertainer one day.

Hard to believe but I was pretty shy most of the time. I didn't used to be the kind of kid who reached out to other people first—until I started playing soccer and went to church camp. I loved singing church camp songs. For me, singing was when I felt most comfortable. As soon as that first note came out of my mouth,

I immediately felt more confident in myself. I sang for anyone who asked me to—like kids at my lunch table—and even when nobody asked! I had no fear. At my cousin's wedding, when I was nine, I asked the DJ to play "Baby" by Justin Bieber and I sang the entire song for the guests. Everyone was jamming and singing. My parents had no idea I was even going to do that. It was awesome. I knew right there that I wanted to be a singer.

In sixth grade, in my school talent show, I sang Bruno Mars's "When I Was Your Man" but added my own special twist. At the end, I handed a rose to a girl in the audience and it worked like a charm. Everyone freaked out. It was the talk of the school for a while. I think people were surprised I could sing! It taught me a big lesson about how to market myself. By eighth grade, I got voted "most talented" in my class. Around that time, I taught myself how to play guitar watching videos on YouTube. I made covers, like "I'm Yours" by Jason Mraz, and posted fifteen-second clips on Instagram. I streamed live on YouNow and sang Ed Sheeran songs like "Thinking Out Loud." In a year, by the time I was a freshman in high school, I shot up from twenty followers on Instagram to 30,000.

School was not interesting to me. I mean, I did well, but literally my mind was always on music. I would get into trouble for tapping my pencil to make sick beats. I would beat my hands or pencils on everything! It got annoying to people! My parents knew I needed music as an outlet. They always said I had a great voice and should try to see what could come out of lessons. They didn't have a lot of extra money but they did what they could to send me to Septien Entertainment Group, the artists development school famous for training Demi

"From the start, music was the biggest part of my life."

Lovato, Selena Gomez, and Jessica Simpson. I learned how to write music and release my own singles. They got me gigs performing at local venues, including Six Flags. Septien helped give me the confidence to be able to get out there and do my own thing. Huge thanks to my teachers and mentors there.

I'd learned so much, but I was kind of stuck at a certain level. My parents could have spent a million bucks, but the reality is, you can't really buy your way to the top. To get there, it takes hard work, talent, and, honestly, a little bit of luck. I got lucky. One day, during the middle of my freshman year of high school, I was standing around with a group of kids, when a girl asked me to sing. I did "Stitches" by Shawn Mendes. She recorded it, and I posted it on Instagram. Someone else shared it to Facebook and it just spread like wildfire. In a week, it went viral—15 million views! It was insane!

Things were never really the same again after that.

I went from being "The Singing Kid" to being "The 'Stiches' Kid." I now had 200,000 followers. Everywhere I went in my town, it was all, "Hey, it's The 'Stiches' Kid!" At first I was like, "That's me!" But then I got kind of bummed. I didn't want to just be "The 'Stitches' Kid," I wanted to be Zach Herron. So, I started making more covers and just posting them to see what happened. Instagram singing pages started posting more of my covers. I was trying to figure out how to branch out into other things. I'd been following a lot of other talented kids on the internet, like Corbyn and Jack, and noticed they were doing cool social media tours. That was really big at the time. I saw YouTube videos of them onstage singing to screaming girls. I was like, "I gotta do that!" So I took it

"Zach's grown up a lot since we started the band."
—Jonah

upon myself and wrote the management of the Impact tour. I just sent them a deep-down email, expressing how much I really wanted to join their tour and explaining why I was a perfect fit. I was so surprised and psyched when they responded: "We can try you out. Come join us for an event and let's see where it goes." I was beyond excited, but also worried about convincing my parents to let me do it. Surprisingly, my parents were kind of proud of me for taking the initiative on my own. They spoke with management and decided to give it a try. My dad and I headed to Indy!

My first live show ever was in Indianapolis in front of six hundred people. I met Jack and Corbyn for the first time and they were super nice to me, even though I was the new guy. I sang "Night Changes" by One Direction, "Thinking Out Loud" by Ed Sheeran, and one of my own songs that I wrote in eighth grade called "Timelapse." The guys liked my set, the audience went crazy, and I even made money selling my merch! Not a bad night! Even better, they put me on the official Impact Spring Break Tour. My whole family came with me—they managed my website and merch—but that's when I really connected with Jack and Corbyn. We always jammed together and got really tight.

I did more social media meet-and-greet tours. My parents took turns traveling with me for days or even weeks sometimes. It was tough on them because I have a little brother and sister, too. I felt bad that they had to be dragged everywhere, but it turns out they really enjoyed it and had lots of fun!

When the opportunity for WDW came about, I was only fifteen. I had other opportunities being offered to me, but being with these guys felt so right. My parents did whatever it took to make this happen. My dad flew out to LA with me, and from then on, it's just been a whirlwind. I was more excited than scared. I knew this was my dream and could feel that it was about to come true! I was so sad, though, to be away from home for so much of the time. I'd miss out on hanging with my friends, just doing teenage stuff. I hated to miss out on spending time with my brother and sister and being a part of their everyday lives. I'd miss out on family game/movie nights and normal everyday stuff, like going to football games and school dances.

It was a huge sacrifice, but I had the chance to live my dream. I couldn't let that go or I'd always regret it. I also worried if I was mature enough to make good choices. I was diving into the ultimate snake pit, the music business in Hollywood. Would I be able to deal with all the crazy stuff thrown at me? Was I strong enough mentally to get through it on my own? My parents had my back, no matter what, and I knew that. They would never let me go down a dangerous path. They would do anything for me and that made me feel safe.

I'd have to grow up fast, but I thought, "BRING IT ON." The fearless part of me didn't realize just how hard it would be at first. It took a lot of getting used to being the young one in the group. I'm two to three years younger than all of them. That's like a sophomore hanging out with college kids, you know? I had to figure out my own way.

The weird part is that I'm the oldest sibling in my family, so it was a huge change for me. I have a younger brother, Ryan, and he really looks up to me. I could always get him to do anything I wanted, like playing "tornado" in the house and

"I really relate to Zach a lot. He is so funny and we are always laughing together."
—Jack

wrecking everything. I came up with the craziest ideas and Ryan always went along for the ride. So it was hard to all of a sudden be in the little bro role with the band and feel like my voice wasn't being heard. I realized a lot of it was just me overthinking things. It's not that they weren't listening to me. It's that there were now five of us with ideas and I had to learn that mine weren't always going to be the best. I looked up to the other guys, so I saw it as an opportunity to learn from them. I had to get used to being the young one and just embrace it. Once I just acted like myself, everything fell into place. The guys and I are really close. Just like real brothers. We spend a lot of time together and talk through things all the time. I don't know what I'd do without them, really. I was ready to

work hard to make it in LA, even if it wasn't going to be easy. Anyone who knows me knows I'm super driven and focused. Nothing was going to derail my dream. My mind was made up—and there was no stopping me.

- - - - - - - - - - - - - - - -

"Zach is a very compassionate and thoughtful person. He genuinely cares about people. He doesn't have one mean bone in his body! I've never ever seen him be mean or ugly to anyone."—Zach's mom

WHO, WHAT, WHEN, WHERE, WHY

PERSONAL MOTTO:

"Be yourself."

PERSONAL THEME SONG:

"Purpose" by Justin Bieber

CHILDHOOD NICKNAME:

My mom used to call me "Peanut," Zachy, or, when she was mad, Zachary Dean.

CELEB CRUSH:

I really like Emma Watson, the actress in *Beauty and the Beast*.

FAVE BINGE:

I like to watch YouTube back at the house after the day is done. I just go sit on the couch with Jack and Corbyn and we watch funny videos.

FAVE FOOD:

I really like pizza but not just any pizza. I have a specific Domino's order: I get crunchy thin crust with beef and ranch dressing. It's not pizza unless I have my ranch.

FAVE HOME-COOKED MEAL:

My dad's breakfast burritos. I will wake up early for them, which is saying a lot because I am not a morning person.

LEAST FAVE FOOD:

Shrimp and lobster. No, I don't like seafood.

HOW I DE-STRESS:

Play video games, go shopping, FaceTime my parents, and SLEEP!

BIGGEST SPLURGE:

The first thing I ever bought when I first got paid was a Louis Vuitton wallet. My number-one biggest purchase was a Louis Vuitton backpack.

FAVE HOLIDAY:

Halloween! I go back home to see my friends and we do this thing every year where we dress up scary, sit on our lawn, act like statues, and scare people. I love my hometown friends. They all sleep over and we watch horror movies and stuff our faces with Flamin' Hot Cheetos, just like old times.

DREAM VACATION:

The Bahamas

BROKEN BONE:

When I was seven, I got on a motorized scooter that my cousin got for Christmas and I was so excited. I jumped on it but I didn't know how to stop. My dumb self didn't just jump off. I hit a curb and the handlebars smashed every bone in my nose. Blood gushed out like a fountain. I had a cast on my nose all of second grade. You can still see the hole.

IF I WAS PRESIDENT:

I would never be president.

FAVE ANIMAL:

A beaver. I just made that up.

HIDDEN TALENT:

I'm a decent artist! I can draw and sketch.
I got that from my dad.

BIGGEST QUIRK:

I'm super analytical and methodical, and plan everything out. Basically, I'm an overthinker! I think way too hard about everything! From social media posts to what shoes I'm going to wear. But being an overthinker has led me to make some great decisions that got me where I am today.

#1 FAN:

Definitely my little sister, Reese. She's only seven and she calls me Zachy. She gets very jealous when she hears other girls say they love me. She always tells me she loves me more!

LEAST LIKE ABOUT MY APPEARANCE:

I'm really pale. I really hate that. But girls really like my smile a lot.

IF I WASN'T A SINGER I'D BE:

A firefighter. I always liked dressing up in uniforms!

BEST ADVICE I EVER GOT:

My dad always tells me, "Stay true to yourself. Don't let anyone make you be who you aren't" and "Don't change so people will like you. Be yourself and

WACKY ZACHY

1. I don't like soda.

2. I love being scared, whether that's watching horror movies or going on the most terrifying roller coaster.

3. But I'm really afraid of elevators! I get claustrophobic.

4. I am super sentimental. My room is like a museum because I won't let my mom clean anything. I like to keep everything that holds a special memory.

5. I want to be an ice-cream truck driver one day.

CHAPTER 4

THE OLD SOUL
Jonah

"Jonah is definitely the big brother. You can talk to him about anything and he'll make you feel good about it."
–Jack

Life can change on a dime.

Ever since I was a kid, I'd been convinced I was going to be a major league baseball player. I was a good pitcher with a nasty curve ball, so I made varsity when I was a freshman in high school. I played on club teams that won tournaments all over the country—crazy enough, one of my teammates just got signed to a multi-million-dollar contract with the Seattle Mariners. Baseball was my plan A; plan B was to be a singer/songwriter.

At the end of freshman year, everything changed. My mom got diagnosed with breast cancer and a lot of my family's energy went to taking care of her. And my parents had to travel to downtown Minneapolis for her chemo treatments. To keep my mind off the seriousness of what my mom was going through—it made me so sad to see her so weak—I gravitated to the internet.

"Growing up, there was always music and laughter in my house."

Every dark cloud has a silver lining. Because of that difficult situation, I spent more time in front of my computer. It was the era of Vine and YouTube, and I saw all these kids blowing up online. I thought that was really cool and wondered, "How do I get in on this?"

I already could sing and play piano. Even though baseball had always been plan A, music came so naturally to me. My mom says from the age of one and a half I mimicked sounds from animals and birds, or from the radio. I knew who my parents were calling on the phone by listening to the melody of the tones they dialed. I was super sensitive to sound all around. In kindergarten, there was a fire drill, and I cried and had to leave. After that, they had to warn me before there was going to be a fire drill! One time at a hockey game, the buzzer went off and I couldn't handle it.

My natural music talent wasn't an accident; it's in my blood. My dad had a band with his brother that played in local churches and clubs near my hometown of Stillwater, Minnesota, as well as playing all kinds of gigs around the world. I'm not super religious but I would go to church a lot and hang out backstage to watch him sing a variety of music ("Come Thou Fount of Every Blessing" was my favorite). No doubt, my dad is my biggest mentor. I always had a fascination with his music and I'd listen to all of his CDs on repeat. I could tell what he was doing was very meaningful to him and his loyal fan base.

Everyone in my family sings, we were kind of like the von Trapp Family Singers. My dad, mom, brother, two sisters, and I sang together a lot in churches, fairs, wherever we could, even when there was no stage! Like, one time we were traveling through Aspen, Colorado, and decided to busk on a corner outside a

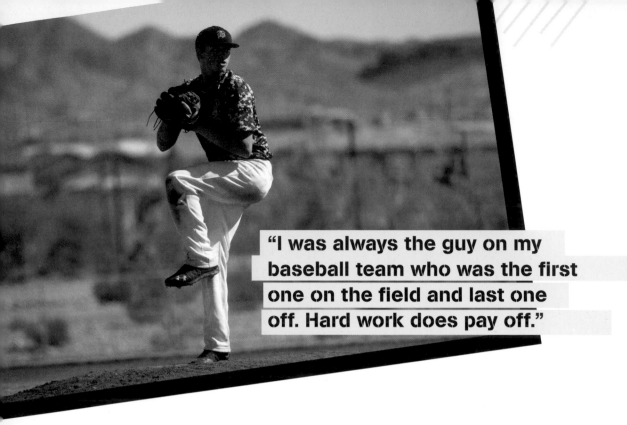

"I was always the guy on my baseball team who was the first one on the field and last one off. Hard work does pay off."

bakery. My dad played guitar and we sang Jason Mraz's "I'm Yours" (I guess all us guys loved that song!). I stepped out and sang a verse, and the open guitar case filled up with coins, bills, and gift cards for muffins! I like muffins.

I'm glad I had that upbringing because I think that's what made a music career even a possibility in my mind. Like the other guys, I taught myself to play instruments and to sing watching YouTube videos, like "Down" by Jay Sean. In sixth grade, I did my first talent show, playing piano to "Imagine" by John Lennon. It was a huge deal and I had major butterflies.

I was in the popular group with the jocks, which was all right, I guess, but looking back I wish I'd had a smaller friend group. It would've been a better experience for me. Everyone wanted to fit in and be in the popular group but what mattered more to me was having real relationships. I had a lot of friends but not many of those relationships felt very real. I'm an athlete but I'm a little more sensitive than the stereotypical jock and, if it isn't obvious, come from a peace-loving family. I mean, my dad sang and my mom is a midwife. They raised us to love our neighbors and nature. My idea of happiness back then was a long walk in the woods with my dog Huckleberry (RIP, buddy). Whenever I go on a hike now, it centers me and brings me back to my roots. That's how I clear my mind.

So, even though I was in the "cool" group, I never felt like I fit in. It wasn't until my mom got cancer and I went on the internet to make music that I found my people. My first broadcast on YouNow only had twenty viewers but every time I logged back on, more and more people tuned in. It snowballed and by ninth grade I had 60,000 viewers. To me that was like selling out Target Field (the Twins' stadium) every night!

Through social media, I was able to find a community and I felt really accepted. It meant the world to me that they liked what I was doing and saying and singing. They were into it and I was inspired to keep creating. Meanwhile, my parents were so preoccupied with my mom's treatments, they had no idea what I was up to, until one morning I came downstairs and said, "Did you know that fifty-six thousand people watched me last night?"

"Watched you do what?" my mom said.

"Sing and play piano."

Then they knew.

Halfway through tenth grade, I left my high school to pursue music full-time. My first live performance ever was in front of 7,000 people at DigiFest. I was freaking out. I went from playing in my room with a piano in front of a computer screen to performing on a huge stage! I got a good response, though, and it led to more social media tours, and that's where I met Corbyn, Jack, and Zach. I'd developed enough of a supportive, loyal following that I put out my own EP of five songs and did a solo tour. I only played for 150 people per night but I loved the intimacy of those shows. I loved the passion of my audience.

I was so honored and humbled to provide music that made the audience happy. Or maybe it helped them deal with hard times, too. I know how that feels. When my mom was sick, connecting with my favorite artists got me through those darkest days. Fortunately, my mom is now a cancer survivor/thriver!

When you're in the middle of something challenging, it's hard to see that anything positive can come from it. I've learned to trust that sometimes it can. To help ease the pain of what was going on in my life, I turned to music. I think that's the biggest reason why I'm on a stage and not a baseball field right now. Some may call that fate, but, to me, it's more mystical. Music is magic.

"If there's ever a rough time, we can go to Jonah and ask him for advice. We always turn to Jonah."
—Corbyn

I may be the quiet one, but my eyebrows do all my talking for me!

PHOTO #1:
When someone calls instead of texts

PHOTO #2:
When I find out a girl loves Wizards of Waverly Place as much as me

PHOTO #3:
When Starbucks spells my name "Johanna" on my coffee cup

PHOTO #4:
When Zach farts on the bus

PHOTO #5:
When I forget to pack enough socks

PHOTO #6:
When I see fifty girls running toward me

The Old Soul—Jonah / in the limelight

PHOTO #7:
When I lose the hotel room key… again

PHOTO #8:
When a fan DMs me a pic of my butt

PHOTO #9:
When I eat raw fish

PHOTO #10:
When I play air sax

WHO, WHAT, WHEN, WHERE, WHY

FAVE MOVIE:

My favorite movie right now is *About Time*—it has time travel in it but it's still a love story. I mean, come on, Rachel McAdams is in it!

FAVE BINGE:

How I Met Your Mother

PERSONAL THEME SONG:

"Eye of the Tiger" gets me pumped up.

FAVE APP:

Twitter, because I have direct communication with the fans and you can post ten times a day. If you do that on Instagram, it's annoying.

BIGGEST SPLURGE:

Before I joined the band, I made a little money touring, so I bought a brand-new red Camaro. I always wanted one. But it's just sitting at my parents' house in Minnesota. I need to get it out to California so I can drive it to the beach!

MOST OVERUSED EMOJI: Winky face

CELEB CRUSH: Camila Cabello

The Old Soul—Jonah / in the limelight

FAVE HOLIDAY:

Fourth of July. I love the middle of the summer. My whole family goes swimming off the point. We have bonfires and couzie-fests and fireworks, good food, lots of chips and salsa.

FAVE CEREAL:

Fruity Pebbles

BIGGEST FEAR:

Tornadoes—they freak me out!

BIGGEST IDOL:

Paul McCartney

LEAST LIKE ABOUT MY APPEARANCE:

No one specific thing. I wish I could be a little more confident in general. I get really shy in certain situations and I don't know why.

MOST TREASURED POSSESSION:

My dad painted me a really cool picture of a house near a lake and a big mountain.

FAVE FOOD:

Thai

FAVE ANIMAL:

Tiger

BIGGEST QUIRK:

I'm a little superstitious. I think that comes from playing baseball. I could never step on the foul line.

IF I WAS PRESIDENT:

I'd solve hunger in the US and all over the world. There shouldn't be any kind of hunger. People have so much, we need to spread it out.

"Jonah is wise like Gandalf."
—Daniel

BONUS JONAHZ

1. My mom's nickname for me as a kid was Jonah Bug.

2. I didn't have a cell phone until ninth grade.

3. I hate cottage cheese, horseradish, and raisins.

4. I can knit, and I make some nice hats (I also know how to cross-stitch, crochet, and quilt).

5. I hate horror movies.

6. In third grade, I broke my nose sledding.

7. I learned to read from baseball cards. I spent one summer memorizing all of the facts on 650 cards!

8. As a tiny kid, I loved vacuum cleaners. My favorite gift when I was two was a Dustbuster. I called it my "baccoon."

9. One time I told my mom I was giving up "salad and church" for Lent.

10. I'm a decent cook, especially breakfast. My specialty is eggs.

CHAPTER 5

THE MUSICAL GENIUS
Daniel

**"Daniel is a good guy and a good friend. You know his heart is always in the right place."
—Jonah**

Here's the first truth about second chances: They rarely happen by chance.

I can't lie—I stole that line from Oprah.com after I googled "second chances." I'm sorry, Oprah! But she's right and it's so true. You don't always get things right the first time around in life. What's most important is you learn from that mistake and don't mess it all up again.

Why Don't We is my second chance. My first chance was making it onto the fourteenth season of *American Idol*. I'd been playing music ever since I stole my sister's pink Barbie piano when I was four and played "Twinkle, Twinkle, Little Star" by ear. My whole life I was obsessed with *Idol*, so it was an out-of-body experience to perform on that stage for millions, get recognized on

the street, be called "beyond adorable" by Jennifer Lopez, get guitar tips from Keith Urban, and crack jokes with Ryan Seacrest.

When I got voted off after Top 9, I was devastated but I deserved it. The truth is, I didn't take it seriously. I'm embarrassed to admit I didn't work that hard. I was only fifteen and having too much fun to care. I was kind of a little twerp.

The night I got booted, I was crying in my dressing room with my family when judge Harry Connick Jr. popped by to see me. "I usually don't do this," he said, "but I want to say that this guy has a light about him that's really special. The way you handled yourself when you got voted off was really inspiring." He gave me his number and told me to keep in contact.

In the early days of *Idol*, the Top 10 went on tour. By the time I got there, they sent the Top 5. So, after living like a rock star for almost a full year on *Idol*, I slunk back to my hometown of Vancouver, Washington, to normal life.

It's like that saying about the grass always being greener on the other side. When I was on *Idol*, I was so homesick. I actually was annoyed being on a TV show. Then when I got home, after two weeks, I was like, "What was I thinking?" I missed *Idol* life so much and I'd totally taken it for granted.

For the next year, I struggled with depression. I'd made it out of the Couve— what locals call Vancouver—only to go right back to where I was before I left. My phone was not blowing up. Nobody offered me a recording contract or a spot on

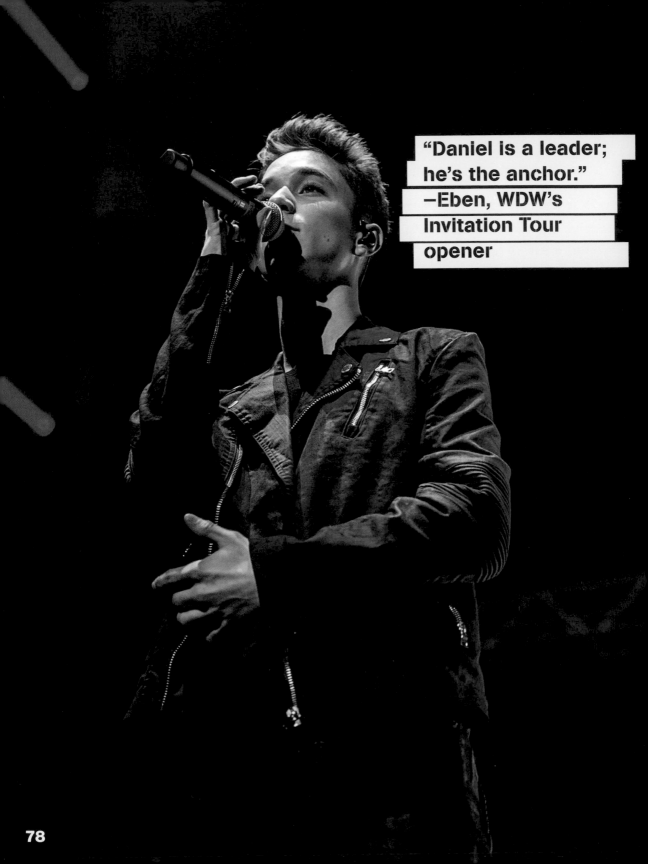

"Daniel is a leader; he's the anchor." —Eben, WDW's Invitation Tour opener

Dancing with the Stars, haha. I was taunted by my classmates, who reminded me on a daily basis that I was a loser. Literally. I felt trapped and hopeless.

I was so clueless about what to do with my life. I was about to chuck my music equipment and apply for a job at PacSun, when my parents stepped in. In a loving yet tough-love kind of way, they said that God had given me a gift, but that I had to work hard for it. Nothing would ever be handed to me again, like *Idol* was.

Except then, weirdly out of the blue, Harry Connick Jr. called me. He was playing a show in nearby Portland and wanted to know if I'd open for him. Um, OF COURSE. I did Hall & Oates's "You Make My Dreams Come True," a song I'd done on *Idol*. After his set, he asked me, "If your family is cool with it, want to come on the road?" I freaked out. I'd never been on the road and I didn't have anything packed. My mom and dad were like, "YES, GO." That night, Harry brought my sister and me to Target and bought us a ton of clothes and supplies. We toured with him for two weeks, down the whole West Coast from Idaho to California. Every day he taught me something new—music theory or jazz or why he never played the same set twice. It was one of the happiest times of my life and super inspiring.

Thanks to Harry, I was back in the business and I wouldn't dare take it for granted ever again. Playing those shows reminded me how much I loved playing music. I got to see firsthand how happy music can make other people and the chance it gives you to touch other people's lives. From that day forward, I vowed to work my butt off to make my music career happen.

From the day I was born, my mom says I had perfect pitch and heard music in everything. Once, when I was six, she wet my bed head with a spray bottle and I said I heard Beethoven's "Ode to Joy" in the spraying sound. In fifth grade, I switched from violin to cello in my orchestra class without telling my parents because they'd just bought me an expensive violin. I didn't even own a cello but I made first chair. To practice, I played the "air cello" in my bed at night.

My idea of a good time was browsing the local music store. I was like a kid in a candy shop and I'd walk around in a daze trying everything out. People would stop to listen and call me a prodigy. My parents bought me every secondhand instrument they could afford: drums, saxophone, banjo, bass. Within hours, I could play songs on any of them. Sometimes I stayed up all night, in this zone oblivious to the time, until I accidentally woke everyone up playing stuff too loudly. My parents would come into my room bleary-eyed and order me to get some sleep.

By the time I was ten, I could play piano and guitar, and sing covers or original songs I'd written. I was deeply influenced by my parents' eclectic taste in music. My dad liked harder stuff by P.O.D. and Falling Up, but my mom loved the ladies lite—Norah Jones, Adele, and Madonna.

I played a few talent shows, singing "Hey, Soul Sister" by Train because I hadn't gone through puberty yet and my voice was still so high. That's when my dad, whose nickname was "Tone Deaf Jeff," was like, "When did you start singing so good?" and took me to Portland's First Friday Art Walk to busk down by the waterfront. He borrowed speakers and a keyboard from our church, and my very first song was Adele's "Someone Like You." I was so nervous and into the music, I looked down, until I heard my dad yell, "Daniel!" I lifted my eyes and saw about three hundred people around me. I had literally stopped traffic!

I'm not saying all of this to brag. I'm just saying this to explain that I had to dig deep to rediscover my passion and purpose in life. When you're doing what you love, you have to remind yourself that you are doing what you love. I was really tested by that and now I always have it in the back of my head.

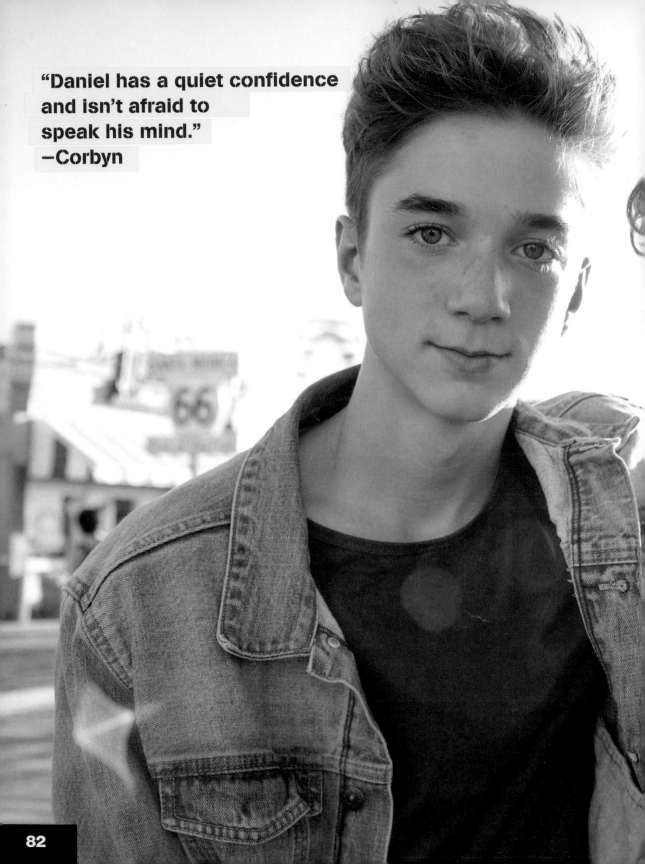

"Daniel has a quiet confidence and isn't afraid to speak his mind."
—Corbyn

Once I looked back at my life and had that aha moment, there was no stopping me moving forward. After the Harry Connick Jr. tour, I was reborn. I got serious about music again and networked like crazy. I played local shows and auditioned for anyone who let me. Nothing felt exactly right, but I'd show up to the opening of an envelope if it would help me reach my goals.

That's how I met Jack, on some weird audition for a nonexistent show in New York. I met Jonah through a mutual friend from Portland. I watched Corbyn kill it online and we DM'd. Zach was the only one I didn't know very well but I had seen his viral video of "Stiches" and thought he was a total star.

By the fall of 2016, all the other guys had met up in LA and were trying to start a band. But it wasn't working out, it wasn't gelling, and they were about to call it quits and go back to their solo careers. Right before they threw in the towel, Jack brought my name up to Corbyn, Zach, and Jonah.

"What about Daniel?" he said.

"Go for it," they told him.

Jack and I were good friends but lived almost across the nation from each other, so it wasn't every day that I would hear from him. The fateful day he reached out to me, my phone was broken. The week before, I was on vacation in Hawaii and went swimming in the ocean with my phone. So yeah, it was a goner. I went a good week without a phone before the weekend finally came and I had time to drive to the Apple store to get a new one. I'm not kidding, the second I walked out of the store with my shiny new phone, I got a call from Jack. It was crazy. I hadn't talked to him in, like, seven months.

"Yo, man, it's been a while," Jack said. "I have a huge project for you that we're working on. If you want to hop on, I think it'd be dope for you. You want to fly down to LA and hang out?"

A week later, I flew back to Hollywood, where it all began for me. The guys and I got together right away. We all clicked. Personally and musically. They told me my voice was exactly the piece of the puzzle that had been missing. I still get goose bumps thinking about those first days we all sang together

because it's one of those unexplainable things when you know something major just happened and it's beyond exciting.

As soon as I agreed to join the band, Why Don't We became officially official. I got my second chance. Everybody deserves a second chance.

"He just gets so entirely lost in his music because he loves it so much."
—Keri Seavey, Daniel's mom

WHO, WHAT, WHEN, WHERE, WHY

PERSONAL MOTTO:

"Work hard in silence: Let your success be your noise." A lot of people feel like they have something to prove. I just can't wait to inspire people with my music and make them dance. I don't need to tell the world how great I am. If the world wants to tell me that, then I'm going to be super thankful for it.

CHILDHOOD NICKNAME:

Some of the other contestants from my season of *American Idol* called me "the Sponge" because of the way I soaked up advice.

FAVE FOOD:

My mom's fettuccine. It's one of a kind and I miss it.

LEAST FAVE FOOD:

Stuffing. I don't understand the concept, the texture, the taste, nothing. Also, dark chocolate—eww, no.

BIGGEST FEAR:

Laziness. Losing an opportunity because of a dumb choice.

The Musical Genius—Daniel / in the limelight

"There is nothing better than doing what you love."

FAVE QUOTE:

"Love your neighbor as yourself."

HIDDEN TALENT:

I can unicycle. I saw one on Amazon, and when I see something like that (I think it comes from being homeschooled for a little bit), I get really excited. I was like, "I have to learn how to unicycle!" I picked it up fairly quickly.

PERSONAL THEME SONG:

"Twist and Shout" (the version from *Ferris Bueller's Day Off*) or "Happy" by Pharrell. You can't go wrong with that. It's good vibes.

HOW I DE-STRESS:

I call my mom. She talks me through everything.

BIGGEST SPLURGE:

I bought a $5,000 drone. I wanted a smaller one because I didn't want to be that guy with the most expensive drone, but the salesman convinced me to get the one that goes fifty miles per hour, has four cameras on it, and has a tracking device. I'm kind of glad I bought it now. I stick it out the window on the tour bus and let it fly. It always comes back!

FAVE HOLIDAY:

Summer break. I very much disliked school. My family went to an island on the Columbia River every day. We had a cheap ski boat that we would use to go wakeboarding and tubing.

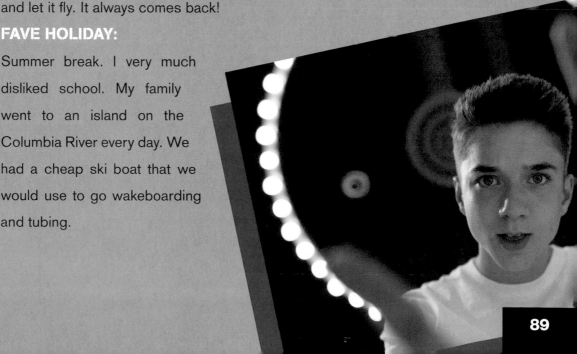

IF I WASN'T A SINGER, I'D BE:

An architect. I geek out when I see a cool bridge.

CELEB CRUSH:

Hailee Steinfeld. I met her at Jingle Ball and, not sure about her, but it was an amazing moment for me.

FAVE ANIMAL:

A lion or a monkey

FAVE CEREAL:

Cocoa Puffs

MOST TREASURED POSSESSION:

My hard drive with all of my music on it. If that thing got lost, I'd be like, DARN.

"My favorite thing about Daniel is the bridge of his nose."
–Zach

CHAPTER 6

Dare to Dream

If you're being bullied, you're not alone. All five of us have been picked on, laughed at, and called names for daring to dream big. For some reason, "fag" is a biggie. We know you're trying to be mean but, fyi, being gay isn't an insult.

It takes a lot of courage to be different and live your life out loud. People get scared of what they don't understand, or, in our situation, mad or jealous that they don't have the same courage or drive to really go for it. We didn't give up and we don't want you to, either. It really does get better—we're living proof of that.

Daniel: Right after I came back from *American Idol*, I was invited to everyone's birthday and Halloween parties. I was like, "Oh, wow, they missed me!" But two weeks later, the hate started and it was brutal. I remember this guy told me about a baseball scholarship he was getting, and how he was really going somewhere and I wasn't. I was taunted in school a lot, with like, "Oh, superstar, what are you doing in geometry right now?" People still say mean things to me. It's sad. I almost feel bad for them because if they really loved something they could do it.

Jack: There were times in school I was picked on a lot for doing me and trying to do music. It's funny, because everyone thought I was really cocky. I was like, "Why does everyone think I'm cocky? I'm just playing guitar." I got the gay comment a lot. Before the perm, I had spiked hair. Everyone would always make fun of me and go, "Hey, three-foot spiked hair!"

Jonah: In high school, I didn't know myself at all. I thought it was cool to hang with the cool kids and that's what made me cool. All my "friends" turned their backs on me when I started live streaming and posting my music on Instagram. When I got 50,000 followers, they weren't happy for me. They were weirded out by it and made fun of me. I'd walk down the hall and the guys would run up to me and scream, "Oh my gosh, it's Jonah!" and take selfies. It was funny at first but after a couple times I realized they were being mean. To them, I was putting myself out there too much. They saw people freaking out about me and they didn't understand it all. Now those same kids text me when I come home, "Hey, let's hang out."

Zach: In seventh grade, I got a lot of followers and I was made fun of for that. I got tons of "Oh, you sing? Sing for us!" But it wasn't in a nice way. It was in a mean, taunting way—I realized that quick. In middle school, everyone is envious when you can sing or have a talent worth being envious of. They really press on that.

Corbyn: I was bullied for sure. I went through a phase in high school where I was very active with my new fans on the internet. I'd post, "You're so beautiful!" or tweet out, "Good night, beautiful girls," that kind of stuff. It wasn't the cool thing to do. For a long time I hated going to school because I got stared down in the hallways, guys would bump into my shoulder on purpose, and I was called a loser and gay. A couple times I tried to play basketball and they'd say, "There are too many people. You can't play." It was envy. They were caught in that "trying to be cool" world and I was caught in that "trying to do what I love" world. I made it through because I knew where my heart was and I knew where I wanted to be. I was making $2,000 per month on YouNow, so I was like, "Suckers! I'm at my house playing music and making money." So that was rewarding for me.

CHAPTER 7

We're All Mama's Boys

Yo, before we move forward, we gotta give a shout out to our biggest fans. Our moms are the best. They've all supported our dreams, even when that meant big sacrifices for our families. To say thanks for all that unconditional love, we had to include them in this book. Plus, they've got more embarrassing stories to tell about us!

Jack & Kristin Stanford

Jack: My mom is the most powerful human in the world. I feel like she's an angel given to me from God. I would not be here today without her. If my mom calls me, I instantly answer. A lot of people take their moms for granted. Your mom is the one who birthed you and sacrificed everything for you. The smallest sacrifice I can make in return is answering the phone and telling her I love her.

Kristin: Luckily there is a thing called FaceTime. I am THAT mom who calls him daily. And I'm pretty lucky he always answers me! I'll never forget the time he was on Radio Disney for an interview and I FaceTimed him. Jack said, "I bet this is my mom." Jack answered and said, "Hey, Mom, we are in the middle of a radio interview right now." Maybe I shouldn't call so often! But I miss him.

I try to get as much quality time as possible when he comes home, but he's very popular! Anytime Jack is in town, I expect to have tons of kids at our house playing cards, or out back playing basketball or skateboarding. He's known as the comedian, always making people laugh. Jack has the biggest heart. He would help anyone if he could. He loves motivating people, pumping them up to be their best self. I'm proud of how thoughtful and sweet he is to everyone. But I'm most proud of him remembering to be thankful and he truly embraces being thankful to God.

Jonah & Carrie Frantzich

Jonah: My mom has taught me so much about how to be a good person. On our early tours, she drove my friends and me around in her Suburban, through the night and through snowstorms for long hours. I made sure that when we blasted our music, all the lyrics were the "clean" version, out of respect for my mom.

Carrie: I'm most proud of Jonah's integrity— he speaks his mind, and his words and actions are in accordance with his beliefs. In music, I'm concerned about messages of misogyny and materialism. At home, we stress teachings about love, caring for others (especially those less fortunate), and peace. With Jonah's music and writing, I push for clean, supportive lyrics.

We are so proud of who Jonah is and who he is becoming. He loves people. He is super social. He is joyous and passionate, and loves to share his life with others. Jonah adds laughter and mischief into the mix. He has always been super social and athletic. He is very comfortable with everyone of every age, gender, and ethnicity. As a child, he would buzz around and engage everyone in conversation about baseball, music, snowboarding, skateboarding, really anything. He was so comfortable, but he had some boundary issues. . . . Once, when he was five, we were in an airport, waiting for a flight. I looked over and saw him, sidled up to a random woman, talking with her. Absentmindedly, he reached over and started playing with the bracelets on her wrist while conversing. She smiled and chuckled.

Jonah brings people together. He's a sensitive, heartfelt young man. Jonah's message is, "You are beautiful. Your life has meaning. You are loved."

Jonah is a gift to us, and we are grateful.

Zach & Myta Herron

Zach: My mom has always been so loving and has always has been there for me. If I just need to talk to someone, I go to my mom. She's the one I can express anything to and she always makes me feel better.

Myta: We are a super-close family and we all have each other's backs. We will drop everything for each other. I'm also super proud of the man Zach is becoming and how he has handled everything while still staying true to who he is. He is still just Zach and I love that he doesn't let things go to his head. He still comes home and takes the trash out! But now, he actually makes an effort to do it before we ask him to!

Zach is always so sweet! He never lets us leave the house without saying, "I love you." I'll always remember the time that I ran to the store and Zach called me right as I was leaving, just to tell me he loved me and to be careful because it was raining. Zach is also super sentimental. He loves all of our little family traditions and it warms my heart. Like, every Halloween I make a special treat called "Monster Mix." He was sure to remind me not to forget to make it this year (he says it every year!).

Myta's Monster Mix:

Spider legs—pretzel sticks

Ghost noses—marshmallows

Monster teeth—candy corn

Creepy crawlers—gummy worms

Cobwebs—Chex cereal

Bug wings—pumpkin seeds

Troll eyes—M&M's

Daniel & Keri Seavey

Daniel: My mom really prepared me for life. A big thing she taught me was to make serving others a priority. She'd say, "To love others, you have to make them a priority before yourself."

Keri: Daniel is a very loving, selfless, and thoughtful person. He really does get joy in bringing joy to others. It makes him generous in so many ways. Daniel is always building something and losing all of my husband's tools in the process. When he first made a little money from *American Idol*, he had me take him to Home Depot to buy a large set of tools for his dad as a payback for the years of losses!

I am, without a doubt, absolutely and most proud of my son's character, his mature resoluteness to stay humble, positive, and kind through all of the ups and downs in the music industry. I would love to be right there for all of it…the good, the bad, and the ugly! I want to be there to encourage him when he is frustrated or discouraged. I want to experience the highs with him because I truly believe that for anything to be fully enjoyed, it must be shared. Daniel is my buddy. I really enjoy hanging out with him! The hardest part for me has been to just let him go and do it all, independent of us. I had to let go of my strong desire to just keep him close, for my sake.

Corbyn & Saskia Vol

Corbyn: My mom's gone through a lot but she always put others before herself. She's always looking out for my brother, my sister, and me. She's a very strong woman and she always did way too many chores for us, so now I really want to take care of her. I want her to wake up stress-free and have her dream house one day—and a cleaning service scheduled weekly!

Saskia: Corbyn goes through life with integrity and humility. He works so hard and yet he never wants to stop learning. He's so self-driven, and always wants to look things up on his own and soak everything in. At his sixteen-month checkup, the doctor asked, "Can he count to ten?" I said, "Ten? He can count to a hundred!"

Since his dad was gone a lot, it's always been the kiddos and me. Because of that, we have a special bond. Corbyn always says, "I love you," and gives me hugs out of nowhere. Even as a teenager he did, and does, that. All of my children truly are my heart and soul. Last Mother's Day, Corbyn made an unexpected visit home and he and my other kids gave me a beautiful gift. It was a glass heart carved into four puzzle pieces, each piece representing my children and me. It had all of our names etched into it with the message, "Together Forever Family." That's when I knew I was doing okay as a mom.

PART II

ON OUR WAY

CHAPTER 8

Boot Camp

Two months after we all started our journey as Why Don't We, we released our first EP, *Only the Beginning*, which debuted at #15 on the *Billboard* magazine's Heat Seekers Chart. Our fan base grew, and our audience loved our new music, and success seemed to come unexpectedly fast. Part of that was because there was demand out there for a new group, especially an American one. The other part was that the magic that began to define WDW was reflected in our music, our vocals, and our communication with you, our fans (which was always truthful and sincere). Looking back on this period in our lives, we realize that there really is no such thing as "overnight success."

We've never told this part of our story before, and we're opening up about it now because we want you all to know what it took for us to realize our dreams. There are lots of stories flying around about how we actually came together, so here's the truth straight from us:

We were five teenagers with gifts—like our unique vocals—and a hunger to pursue solo careers in the music industry and make a living doing what we loved most: performing in front of legions of fans. We were each starting to get some traction on social media platforms like Instagram, Facebook, Twitter, etc., and were doing different digi tours with other social media musical artists. At the

same time, there were two guys in Los Angeles with amazing résumés who were at the top of their careers in the music business, having worked closely with Justin Bieber, Justin Timberlake, Jennifer Lopez, Usher, Lionel Richie, Prince, and Michael Jackson (to name a few). They decided the time was right for an American group of talented teenage boys to burst onto the scene. You could say the timing was perfect for the seven of us—or you could say it was just destiny.

The two LA guys were David Loeffler, a former artist in a successful group and an accomplished talent manager, and his legendary partner, Randy Phillips. They were contacted by an old friend from high school, Jon Lucero, who ran Brave Fest, where a couple of us had performed as solo artists. Initially, Jon contacted Jack, Corbyn, Jonah, and Zach. With financial assistance from Jack's uncle, the four of them flew out to LA to perform as a group for David and Randy.

Then Jack DM'd Daniel Seavey and asked him to fly down to Los Angeles. As he mentioned back at the beginning of the book, Daniel had experienced a taste of Hollywood when he was a top-ten finalist on the second to last season of the original *American Idol*. At that point, though, Daniel was contemplating going to college to become an architect. But once he arrived and started to rehearse with the four of us, it was like the heavens opened up and the birds began chirping like some kind of Disney movie. We started harmonizing and realizing all these crazy things we could do together vocally. We went back to perform for David and Randy again, and it took only about five minutes for everyone to realize this was it!

Even if none of us truly remembers how the name Why Don't We became official, we knew we were going to ride or die together as we began this journey. We made a deal with David, Randy, and a third business partner—digital content delivery entrepreneur Steve Miller—that, no matter what, the five of us would have a voice in all decisions affecting the group, including the songs we recorded, the venues we played, our image, our wardrobe, communication with our fans, and even the title of this very book you're holding (after all, someone had to reject the title "Why Don't We Read This"). Authenticity is really important to us and we wanted to make sure that no matter how big we got, we still felt and acted like ourselves.

David promised us that within two weeks of signing with him and Randy, we'd drop new music on iTunes and Spotify. That was unheard of in the music business, especially considering that we did this as independent artists without a major record label behind us. David promised us that he could make us more successful than we ever dreamed, but the caveat was that we had to do everything that he asked, even if it sounded crazy. His plan was to merge all our individual fan bases and release great new music constantly and digitally. An integral part of this plan was to tour as soon as humanly possible, do VIP meet and greets, and create a really cool merch line. "Hit 'em hard and often" was David's mantra—and don't focus on record deals and radio airplay, which would come in due time. This groundbreaking strategy seemed a little nuts and almost impossible, but we trusted him. After all, what did we have to lose?

To execute this plan, our managers moved the five of us into this contemporary glass house (owned by Randy) on a plateau overlooking Los Angeles, where we engaged in a practically military-style boot camp sans the mud, sand, and guns. Instead, we trained with microphones and worked on perfecting our live vocals, performance training we called "groove therapy," stage presence, physical conditioning, and media training. Together, we recorded the songs and created the sound that defined WDW. There was a degree of blood, sweat, and tears, as the cliché goes, but nobody actually bled (unless we were popping a zit)!

Inside the house, David installed a mobile recording studio in the dining room using one of the bedrooms as a vocal booth. He got a killer writer/producer team, Troy "R8DI0" Johnson and Candice Pillay, to work with us on original material. True to David's word, within two weeks we released our first song, "Taking You," in the fall of 2016. And within two months, we released our first EP, *Only the Beginning*, and headed out on our first North American tour. In a year, we knocked out four more EPs and grew our fan base into a worldwide phenomenon.

Seems so simple, right? Nope. Wrong. It wasn't. That first year, we went through an intense training process that tested us as professionals. Our families and friends were temporarily put on hold while we recorded, rehearsed, and toured. We worked long days, sometimes logging eighteen hours. We lived in this beautiful house in the hills, but it was not large and the five of us slept

in two bedrooms; Jack and Daniel on air mattresses in one room, Jonah, Zach, and Corbyn in the other.

House rules were: we had to wake up by 10 a.m. (not easy

for five teenage boys!) and, at one point in the process, we were required to put our phones down by 10 p.m. (almost impossible for five teenage boys!) and go to sleep by midnight. On one hand, it was the coolest thing any of us had ever done. On the other hand, it was exhausting. The results, however, were exhilarating. And we learned one lesson very quickly: hard work can really pay off even if it means working 24/7 to get there.

We were five individuals who decided to sacrifice some of the normal teenage coming-of-age experiences to pursue our dreams. There was stress and the uncertainty of not knowing whether this sacrifice would work, there were disagreements and fights, a lack of privacy, tears and laughter. I think our parents and families wondered if we had lost our minds. Ultimately, though, we had each other and knew in our guts that this was right and that magic was being created. You have heard of "trial by fire"—well, we became "brothers by fire" and formed a strong bond that our fans know is real.

We were pushed to the extreme to sing better, be more creative, dig deep to create more great content, look great, and sound great. Once we made peace with David's drive and the method to his madness, we stopped whining and trusted the process. For example, groove therapy became a daily morning ritual where we blasted music. Drake's "Passionfruit" was big at this time, and we literally grooved to that and other songs, which gave us confidence in our movement and stage presence.

"These are the hardest-working teenagers in show biz."
—Bam Bam, tour manager

"We are all in this together. We are partners."
—Randy Phillips, co-manager of Why Don't We

Just like Randy and David promised, radio stations like KISS FM (the number-one station in Los Angeles), Z100 in New York City, and many of the largest pop stations in the country started playing our song "Something Different" even without the backing of a major label. *Forbes* magazine wrote that we were the "Next 1D" and analyzed our growing social media followers and, more important, our growing fan engagement. We were featured in *Rolling Stone*, *Billboard,* and *People*, to name a few of the publications featuring the "WDW phenomenon." YouTube superstar vlogger Logan Paul discovered us online and directed the music videos for "Nobody Gotta Know" and "Something Different" and codirected the "These Girls" video.

That year in the house in the hills was the hardest of our young lives. It was such a long shot we'd make it, but we did (at least, we are on our way!). If it wasn't for that boot camp, we would not be here today, which means:

We now have real stage presence and confidence in our live vocals, so we can give our fans a killer live experience.

We're all brothers. Since we were away from our families, we had to be there for each other. Living in that house for a year in such close quarters made us so tight. We've worked hard together, we've cried together, we've laughed together, and we've fought together. However, we now know how to work things out together.

We made a sick deal with Atlantic Records! A year after we formed, the major labels couldn't ignore the Why Don't We buzz and practically beat down our door. Randy negotiated a groundbreaking deal for a new artist in the music industry, and we have a wonderful creative and business relationship with Atlantic, the number-one market-share label in the industry. BOOYAH!

We now have our own WDW house in Hollywood! We have a whole place to ourselves! We got to a point where we were ready and our managers could tell we were ready. We yearned for our own space and it worked out for us in the end and it is amazing!

We are a professional band. We have discipline, but we still have fun. We've been exposed to so many new experiences and have traveled the world. We know how to meet people, answer questions in interviews, interact socially, and step into the role of an artist and entertainer. Most of all, we love our fans who got us here.

Whenever we need to get motivated, we think back to those times when we were really pushed to be on top of our game. It's what you need to succeed in this career because it is a lot harder than people think. It's not just glitz, screaming fans, and glamour—behind the scenes it is so much more. As we said earlier, there is no such thing as "overnight success," but we wouldn't trade places with anyone else and will never take our fans or our success for granted.

JACK'S THREE POINTS FOR SUCCESS

1. Work as hard as you possibly can. No matter how hard it is, just do it. If it's 4:00 a.m. and you have to be up at 6:00 a.m., you still work. Sleep is for the weak. Us guys don't sleep. We work all the time. If you multiply the work you put in now, the results multiply. I truly believe that.

2. Stay motivated. What you do now matters later. Be patient. You're not going to see results in an hour—it could take months or years.

3. Always be nice to others. Always be happy because that makes other people happy and that makes everyone happy in general!

CHAPTER 9

Bro-le Models

Ever since we became a band, everyone wants to know our biggest inspiration. Sorry, we don't have one.

…we have *three*!

Ed Sheeran

Daniel: When I was on *Idol*, they asked me, "What's your unique sound?" I was like, "A jazzy Ed Sheeran." I always looked up to that guy for his songwriting and how he strips everything down to an acoustic guitar. He's an artist but in pop music.

Corbyn: Ed Sheeran is constantly dropping beats and music. It's inspiring for us to see a guitarist and pianist sell out three Wembley Stadium shows in England. He's tapped into something crazy over there.

Jonah: I remember going through a breakup and listening to his *x* album a lot. It really helped.

Jack: I was kind of obsessed with Ed Sheeran. He was the first to influence me to play guitar. I remember him singing and playing guitar and making loops

with his voice. I was like, "Man, he's his own band," so I got a looper and my own guitar, as well. I posted Ed Sheeran covers all the time. My sister posted a picture of him busking when he was little and commented to me, "Jack, Ed Sheeran was busking on the streets and now he's doing stadiums. That's where you'll be one day." It's funny because one time my English teacher said, "I want you to write a story about whatever you want," so I made up a story up about meeting Ed Sheeran and performing with him onstage. I cheated; my sister wrote it for me. She's very talented, so I got a 94 on it."

Justin Bieber

Zach: Growing up, Bieber was the guy to watch. He had the clothes and the shoes to buy. But we never wanted to admit it, because you know...

Daniel: I've done a bunch of Justin Bieber covers and used to get compared to him a lot. We both started out as street performers. I admire that he takes risks and is always pushing his own sound. His style definitely caught my eye. I can't lie—I wore the Supras, too!

Jonah: He's definitely one of my biggest inspirations. I remember being twelve and seeing him perform at Jingle Ball in Minnesota when he was fifteen. It was so cool seeing a kid so young up there. I'd seen my dad perform, but to see someone from my generation do it, it really made me want to do that. I sang a lot of Justin Bieber stuff. When I was in sixth grade, the movie *Never Say Never* came out. I was so blown away by Justin's music and spiritual awakening. I organized an outing for my entire class of sixty kids to go to the opening. I didn't care that most of the other guys didn't think it was cool. I personally called and invited every kid to come and arranged to have people carpool so everyone had a ride. Years later, I heard from a girl named Beth, who never forgot the personal invite. She'd been thinking about quitting school because she'd been bullied, but my phone call encouraged her to stay and reconnect with the other kids.

Jack: Meet and greets can be a little scary but you can't be like, "I'm sad," you have to make

sure you're happy for the fans there because it means a lot to them. Whenever I get drained at meet and greets, I remember how Justin Bieber used to do like six hundred people per night. We only do like 150, so he inspires me to keep going.

Jaden Smith

Corbyn: He wears whatever he wants—he'll wear women's clothing or a dress or put the craziest two pieces together—and you're like, I could never pull that off but it looks THE dopest!

Jack: I wear his line, he's got sick merch, his whole vibe is crazy dope. He's so creative and so artsy and very himself. He lets people know what his brain is thinking, and it's very cool. He wears a dress, like screw it, he just does it. I want to pick his brain and just talk with him.

Jonah: Jaden Smith commented on my Instagram post once, on a picture of all of us announcing that "Trust Fund Baby" had dropped. He wrote, "Flex," which basically meant we were killing it. That made my day.

CHAPTER 10

Setlist

"The first time I heard these guys sing, they blew me away."
—WDW producer Troy "R8DIO" Johnson

It's hard to put into words why we love music so passionately, but we're gonna try:

Daniel: It's visual without being visual. It's like speaking your own beautiful language.

Jonah: It's otherworldly. You can totally disconnect from everything around you and live in it.

Corbyn: I love the science behind it, like why "Da da da" might sound better than "Dah dum dah," and crazy stuff like that.

Jack: There's a freedom to it. You can form your own interpretation—there are no rules.

Zach: It's my happy place.

As hard as that year living at David's was, making music together was always so easy and organic. Right off the bat, we knew how to put all of our voices together on a song. We could be like, "Oh, I hear Corbyn for that! Zach should sing the chorus!" We heard each other's parts and the harmonies. We sang 24/7, wherever we were, we didn't care. Freestyling. Like Jack would pick up a guitar and play really stupid chords, and we'd sing a really stupid melody. We all chimed in, one of us beatboxing, three of us doing harmonies, one singing lead. Then we turned them into songs and voice recorded them on our phones. In fact, there's one we always perform called "Bunga Bunga." We made it in the bathroom late one night when we were all in there together. It's an inside joke now. We do it at sound checks and reference it in interviews sometimes but no one knows what it means! Only we know. We just laugh and now you can laugh with us when you hear it.

Our chemistry was already lit, but when we started working with our Grammy-winning writer-producer team Candice Pillay and R8DIO, who'd worked with Rihanna, Christina Aguilera, Kendrick Lamar, Jay-Z, Backstreet Boys, and Will Smith, they took it to a whole other level. We went to eleven, for all you *Spinal Tap* fans out there! Candice and R8DIO had the freedom to create music that pushed culture and would make an impact on our generation. They'd spend a week together making songs with urban influences, then together with David, who has an incredible ear, pick the best ones for us to record.

Candice and R8DIO masterfully tailored parts in the songs to fit our individual styles so that each voice was different, brilliant, and easily recognizable. Here's how Candice breaks it down, because like she always says, "I know their voices like the back of my hand—I couldn't ask for more diverse beauty in a group!"

- **Zach's voice is "butter," his tone "breathtaking," which suits a lot of our hooks and intro verses.**

- **Jonah has a deep raspy tone, which they use to "talk to the girls."**

- **Corbyn has a "beautiful tone that hits the sweet spots. It's lovely to open our songs."**

- **Daniel has "amazing depth and delivery. His voice is gorgeous and brings our songs to life."**

- **Jack "hits our strong highs and is amazing at vocal runs."**

We got so tight with Candice and R8DIO since, for a year, we ate, slept, and breathed Why Don't We together. They created a recording space that was patient, safe, and nonjudgmental and we just thrived. None of us will ever forget the energy in the studio the very first time they played back our first professionally recorded song, "Taking You," mixed and mastered by our new maestros. Everyone was bobbing their heads and jamming—even David popped and locked! In our first week as Why Don't We, we'd created something special and everyone knew it. We had butterflies. It was the most amazing feeling in the world.

Our fans had supported us as solo artists but we had no idea if they would accept that we were in a group with other guys. Well, when "Taking You" came out, we got our answer. Our EP hit number fifteen on Billboard's Heatseeker chart, and to date, the video has more than 16 million views on YouTube!

In the next year, we dropped new music constantly and our fans loved it. We released five EPs, all produced by R8DIO and Candice. They'd pop over to David's house and we'd sit around in a circle hashing new stuff out. Sometimes they'd come with an idea and we'd go off of that, or we'd come up with it right there. We all played a big part in the creative process and it was heaven. All that blood, sweat, and tears we talked about before finally paid off when our EP *Why Don't We Just* peaked at number two on Billboard's Heatseekers chart.

We'd love to analyze every single song we made but we need a whole other book for that! So here are some of our favorite lyrics:

Corbyn: "Cause only never comes when never's all you know" from "Never Know." I feel like "Never Know" is so underrated. It's the one song we've done that's not necessarily about love; it's about inspiration and pushing forward and following your dreams. "Only never comes when never's all you know" means if you don't ever shoot for the point, you'll never make the goal. It was a really cool way to portray that idea.

"They're stars. You can't teach that, they were born with it."—Candice Pillay

Daniel: "Hollywood girl, tryna be like Rihanna" from "These Girls." I love kinda rapping that part.

Jack: "Wanna free-fall inside your head / Go everywhere you've been / See everything you've seen / So I can understand," from "Runner." That whole verse is so powerful. You're saying to a girl you want to know everything she's thinking. I feel like girls would be like, "Oh, dang, he wants to know me!"

Zach: "I like you, you like me / Let's just get together" from "Invitation." I really like that because it's so simple but it's one of my most popular lines I sing. When I sing it into the crowd, they're like, "Hey, I like you!" It's so funny.

Jonah: "It took a while to figure out / What type of girl that I'm about / Who brings the real man out of me" from "Trust Fund Baby." As soon as I heard that part, I knew I wanted to do it. I just connected to it lyrically. It resonated with me.

THE LYRIC THAT LAUNCHED A FANDOM BY CANDICE PILLAY

"Taking You" was one of the first records R8DIO and I wrote for the band. I played a guitar loop idea for R8DIO, which he embellished on. I remember sitting at the mic; I always sing the first thing that pops into my head and he records it. The best ideas always come when you aren't really trying. I sang, "I need you in my life like limelight," then stopped and said, "That's too silly, right?" His eyes got really wide and he smiled and said, "No, it's perfect!" We never knew that word would end up being the name of the WDW fan club! It's kind of beautiful because the song is about unconditional love and the fans are exactly that for the boys.

We started off making music our way, we took a huge risk, and people started noticing. At the end of 2017, we got a deal with Atlantic Records. The head of our label came to our house and said, "Hey, guys, I have a song for you called 'Trust Fund Baby.' By the way, it was written by Ed Sheeran." It was not only surreal that our hero wrote a song for us; it was a game changer.

Working on our first "real" album was the opportunity of a lifetime. We attended writing camp, or as we called it "Musical Disneyland." An entire recording complex was rented out for us in LA and all seven studios were packed with the biggest and best writers and producers. We played musical studios, bouncing in and out of them, hanging and collaborating when the mood and the material connected. One producer we worked with was Steve Mac, who helped craft Ed Sheeran's massive hit "Shape of You," and has worked with Demi Lovato, One Direction, and Kelly Clarkson.

They have an incredible work ethic. They are humble and listen. The love and heart they put into their music is real."
—Candice Pillay

Our first album with Atlantic Records is due out in the fall of 2018. We think you're gonna flip for "Hooked" and "Friends."

"Hooked" was fun to record because we went far out of our comfort zone. It's got more of a rocker vibe and it leaps and bounds in a way we've never done lyrically before. The tone of our voices is different—Jack even gets to have a cool rasp.

It's a little more edgy, about how a girl kisses your neck, then takes a bite and then there's an apple crunch sound. It's exciting to touch on those things in a cool, catchy way and add some flavor to it. We're teenage guys, so we do have all these feelings.

"Friends" took a minute to warm up to. At first, we were like, "Eh, I don't know," and then by the third time we listened to it, it was like, "THIS IS THE DOPEST SONG WE'VE EVER HEARD." It has Latin vibes and crazy guitar solos with plucking. "Friends" is a song you can play anywhere: at the beach, lying in bed, you can play it RIGHT NOW. It's one of those songs that makes you want to tap your feet. It's a little bit different of a direction, like "Despacito."

With our new album, we took risks because we want to make it to the next level. We want to have the kind of hit single where you wake up one morning and hear the song playing everywhere. We can't wait for that day!

THANK DANIEL FOR THOSE SICK MASHUPS

Daniel is our musical genius. He has perfect pitch and can play any instrument. We practice our mashups until they're perfect, then post them on Instagram.

CORBYN'S DREAM COLLABORATION

Julia Michaels, just because her voice is so unique and so distinct and, you know, it's Julia Michaels. She's super talented and super sweet. I think we could make a really, really cool song together.

Behind the Scenes of Our Videos

We love making our music visual. Some of us (Zach, ahem) like acting
more than others (Daniel, ahem, who doesn't like pretending to be a character). It's a blast coming up with a creative concept and seeing it come to life.
Depending on our mood, sometimes we make them funny or romantic. Other
times, we want the music to be the focus.

One thing we all agree on is that **"Trust Fund Baby"** was our favorite video
to shoot so far. It was shot at Roosevelt High School in Seattle, and directed
by Jason Koenig, who did Ed Sheeran's "Shape of You" video—so that was
pretty major. And the whole song is about independent, strong women, so it's
really relevant to what's going on in the world right now. We loved getting put
in our place by all the amazing ladies in the video, from the professional dance
troupe to the ace who smoked Jonah in the batting cage to the skater girl who
schooled Jack on her skateboard.

Even beyond the empowering message, it was so cool that we all got to experience high school for a day. All of us left our schools early to pursue music, so even though this was just a video, we got to hang out with so many kids our own age. Zach loved it! They'd filled a school bus with extras and Zach hopped on for so long, it actually drove away with him on it! Everyone was like, "Okay, we lost Zach." He had tons of fun and didn't want to get off that bus. It was hard to pull him off!

It was cool to hang out with all the extras. By the end of the shoot, we were all friends. We had one of the most genuinely fun times filming that video. The hype was real!

Our Top 10 Fave Video Moments of All Time

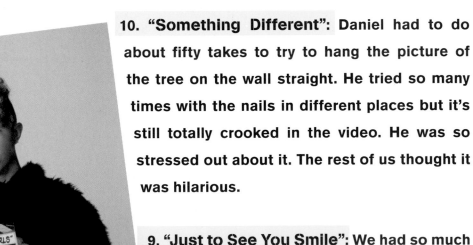

10. "Something Different": Daniel had to do about fifty takes to try to hang the picture of the tree on the wall straight. He tried so many times with the nails in different places but it's still totally crooked in the video. He was so stressed out about it. The rest of us thought it was hilarious.

9. "Just to See You Smile": We had so much fun running all over New York City talking to fans. We didn't have any permits, so it was a guerilla-style shoot. This was early, when we really started to blow up, so it was cool for people to recognize us and hear us sing live and be like, "Wow, you can really sing!"

8. "Taking You": Our very first video shoot was at Milk Studios in LA, which was kind of fancy. We had the whole warehouse to ourselves. We didn't really know how to dance, so one of the scenes is us just standing there with girls' hands all  over our bodies. Daniel's mom was on set and she was cracking up, but we were all beet red from embarrassment.

7. "Craft Services": That's not the name of one of our videos, we just love the free snacks they give us! Jack especially likes the array of beverages, from Sprite to Coke to Dr Pepper, plus all the sweet candy. He wants you to know that's his absolute favorite part of a shoot.

6. "Help Me Help You": YouTube star Logan Paul really championed us early in our career, promoting us in his vlog and this music video, which got 100 million views. We know he made a big mistake, but he always treated us with respect, and we want to thank him for directing four of our videos and helping put us on the map.

5. "These Girls": In Daniel's part, they brought in a pink horse and it took the biggest poop and nobody cleaned it up. So when Jonah came in after to shoot his scenes, it smelled so bad but he didn't know why! Finally someone told him. And cleaned it up.

4. "Nobody Gotta Know": Originally, the first girl we shot was a friend of ours, so it was kind of a fake setup. But Zach really wanted to go up to real girls and hand them roses. And that's how the video ended up with all of us singing for real girls. Zach is so fearless. We were at a restaurant once where the waitstaff was singing "Happy Birthday" to this guy. We dared Zach to go over and sing happy birthday to him, too. He did it and the guy loved it. Ten minutes later, the waiter came over to us and said that he bought us dessert!

3. "Invitation": There are a ton of hidden tributes to the fans in it, like Limelight tea, Zach's snacks, and Bam Bam's name on the Mario Bros. video game.

2. "Trust Fund Baby": The scene where Daniel is driving the blue car with all of us in it, he made a quick turn in gravel and Jack flew out of the car and was dragged while holding the door handle! He rolled away into a train track. Honestly, sadly, we were laughing because we didn't know how to react. If it was anyone else, we would've been scared but we knew Jack would be okay somehow. And he's still alive!

1. "You and Me at Christmas": Who doesn't love cocoa on Christmas morning?!

CHAPTER 11

Style We ❤

BY CORBYN

When it comes to our clothes and accessories, we all get a little competitive. If any of the guys are wearing a dope outfit, we all want to look that dope! Not in a mean way where we want to be better, but it keeps us looking fresh and on our toes.

Being the most stylish guy in the band takes a lot of strategic planning. We aren't at the point yet where we get free expensive stuff sent to us all the time, so we have to pay for it ourselves! We gotta figure out how *not* to wear the same outfits over and over on social media without going broke. When we see stuff we like on Instagram, we DM our lovely costume designer, Teresita Madrigal, and, if we can't afford it, she'll re-create it for us! She's made us the coolest outfits for onstage, like Jack's green suit with the faces of icons like Kurt Cobain, Marilyn Monroe, and Muhammad Ali all over it, or my black-and-white Two-Face concoction.

Here's a breakdown of each guy's looks, according to me, because I think I'm the most fashion-forward. I'm not tryna brag! I just look at fashion in more depth in terms of colors that

go together and the ways different fits contrast or complement each other. The other guys don't really go into the reasons behind it like I do. But we all have very specific tastes and we know what we like. Like, right now we are all into Korean brands like Off-White and Lip Under Point. That could change, though, because our style is always evolving!

Zach:

Who takes the longest to get ready? That's too easy—Zach! He admits that he's an over-thinker, so even though he plans his whole outfits a week in advance, he takes forever putting together his outfits. He's usually debating shoes and shirts but if he's having a bad hair day, that can tack on time, too. He used to be a big hair freak; now he's all about his outfits. Zach has a cool, casual look. He loves layers. He'll wear an oversized shirt with skinny jeans. He likes to shop at

Barneys or Zara or get his pants from a UK brand called Bershka. He loves vintage shopping on Melrose in Hollywood. He's a young guy who dresses like a young guy. It's fairly basic and mostly all black with maybe a colored pair of shoes or maybe a dash of color on his shirt. He does secretly like pink a lot and is dying to wear fur. But a lot of the time, it's just straight black. We all wear black a lot of the time.

Jack:

He's Boho rock 'n' roll. He wakes up, his hair does what it does, and he just throws on clothes and walks out the door. But his style is always fresh and he can pull off a lot of different things. He can wear a lot of color and design and contrast and numbers-on-a-jersey-type stuff. He can pull off ripped jeans, joggers, sweatpants, everything.

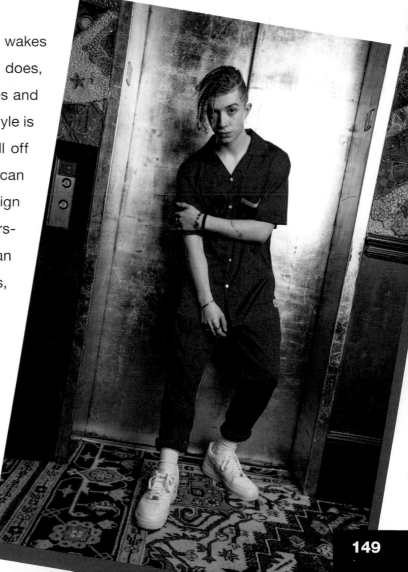

Jonah:

His biggest style influence is G-Eazy. He's got the chill vibe. He has this cool, grungy, laid-back style that goes with his personality. He'll throw on a T-shirt, jeans, and Vans and look super dope. It's like, How do you pull off such a simple outfit and look so good? He's not materialistic at all but he will randomly just show up with the sweetest, most expensive pair of sunglasses, like gold Louis Vuittons. It's so funny, he comes in with this certain walk and always pulls off the craziest pair of shades.

Daniel:

He's gone through a couple different style changes since the band started. He used to wear a lot of button-down shirts but felt like he wanted to dress younger.

He can do the guy-next-door vibe or he can do a more glam Harry Styles look, where he buttons up a shirt with a deep collar, and wears skinny jeans with Chelsea boots. Lately, he's gone a little more skater-ish, in ripped jeans and slip-on Vans. He wears a purple beanie a lot. You can't really guess what he's going to wear the next day. He changes it up!

THE MEN IN THE MIRROR

We're all mirror boys. We don't even realize we're doing it, but if we spot any reflective surface, guarantee we will all stare at ourselves longingly as we walk past. Mirrors are an essential part of our lifestyle and home decor. My room has a closet mirror on the whole door. Jack has a whole sliding-closet-door mirror. Daniel has a mirror wall and Jonah has the master bedroom, so he has a giant mirror. I don't have a mirror wall. Now that I think about it, my mirror sucks!

Daniel likes the mirror a lot, but Zach is the OG mirror hog. If you see any mirrors anywhere, that's where Zach is. If you walk into a place for the first time, Zach will find the first mirror. He will check his look for, no exaggeration, twenty minutes. He does his jaw thing like Zoolander and checks and checks and goes back and forth and gets up close. I gotta give it to him, he works that camera, he's got his angles down! We all throw elbows for mirror space but Zach literally can't walk by a reflective surface without checking himself out. One time we were in a business meeting in London and Zach spent the entire time looking up at the ceiling. We thought he was bored or sleeping but later we realized there was a mirror on the ceiling!

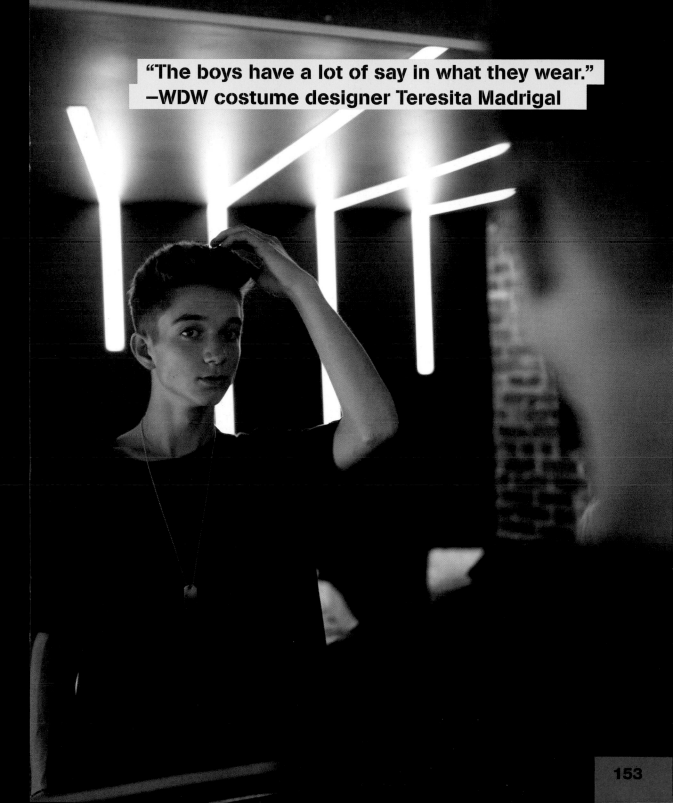

"The boys have a lot of say in what they wear."
—WDW costume designer Teresita Madrigal

CHAPTER 12

Backstage Pass

"These boys are blowing up."
—Reed Benson, stage manager

A month after forming as a band, in the fall of 2016 we went on our very first tour. We'd made some killer music. We'd amassed a solid social media following. It was time to put the two together live! We piled into a ten-seater van driven by Jon, with his wife, Stacy, as navigator, and performed anywhere anyone would let us. Malls, theaters, street corners, a bowling alley bar—wherever we went barely a hundred kids showed up, though one show at an ice cream shop had girls spilling out of the joint. Mmm, cookie-dough ice cream.

The tour was grueling. We drove through the night, a few times in pitch-black snowstorms, to get to our next gig. The van was so crowded with people and equipment, we slept with our knees folded into our chests. It was nuts! But you know what? It didn't matter how many people came, it was THE BEST feeling in the world. It was the first time we experienced the happy vibes of an audience together. We looked at the crowd and saw that our songs were uplifting their spirits. It was like, WOW, they're here for us. It was a total adrenaline rush.

By the time we did our second tour, in the summer of 2017 to promote our second EP, *Something Different*, something major had shifted. We'd booked

larger venues, but still didn't expect much. Our show was still pretty basic, a few flashing lights and five black stools to sit on while we sang onstage. When we arrived at our gig in Buffalo, a huge line of girls was waiting behind a black curtain. When we walked by, they FREAKED OUT. We knew it was going to be an interesting night! When the announcer introduced Why Don't We to start the show, the whole arena exploded in a deafening roar. Everyone knew us. We took out our earbuds to soak in the cheers of the crowd. During the show, we put our mics out and the crowd knew every single word of every song. It was insane.

Back then, our biggest show was 1,500 people in Dallas at the House of Blues. Now our smallest show is 1,500 but we're selling out lots of venues that hold more than 3,000 people! The bigger we get, the bigger and bolder we make our shows with cool choreography, video compilations (of us taking our shirts off, you're welcome), and, of course, our signature original "mashups." We know what our fans like! We even make sure each guy moves to all areas of the stage. Y'all have a favorite you want to see and we are happy to accommodate that!

Touring is such good times. We wish you could experience it, but since you can't be with us 24/7, here's what our pre-show routine looks like through our eyes:

3:00 p.m. Our tour bus pulls up to the venue and we already see crowds lined up to see us five hours before show time. They run to the fence screaming and we wave through the windows.

3:15 p.m. We get off the bus, and if there's a secure parking lot, we take out the

skateboards, motorized scooters, and mini bikes we bought at Walmart and tool around doing wheelies and jumps and ollies. Jack does tricks off the back of our equipment truck, delighting the crowd but worrying everyone else that he will break his leg and the show will be canceled. He lands the jump and is fine. Crisis averted.

3:16 p.m. Jack goes over to the fence to sign autographs on weird things, like bottles of lotion and phone cases, and is humbled to hear sweet fans saying things like, "Why is this man so beautiful?"

3:30 p.m. Sound check. If we want to sing perfect harmonies, we have to warm up our voices. Scales are boring so sometimes we do the "Bunga Bunga" song or "Chicken Fried" by the Zac Brown Band or even make up words to our hits. Like, instead of singing,

"We could be free, we could be free," from "Free," we might sing, "We could eat cheese! We could go pee!" We need to make sure our mics and ears are working perfectly. Daniel takes the lead on our tech fixes. He requests less distortion and more cowbell. Y'all scream so loud, we need to make sure we can hear each other! RIP our ears.

3:35–4:00 p.m. We practice moonwalking. We post random stuff to social media. More scootering and skateboarding in the parking lot while the stage is set up.

4:00 p.m. VIP meet and greet starts. We fan out and talk to every single fan individually. We get polka-dot gift bags with tons of food and socks in them. We take selfies. Zach pretends to propose to a girl. Jack holds hands with a fan. Jonah is asked to prom. Corbyn is gifted an acre of land on the moon (for real!).

Daniel chokes on a Flamin' Hot Cheeto from a gift bag and has to leave for a minute. Everyone freaks out that he won't be able to sing tonight! He gets water. He's totally fine. Crisis averted.

4:30–5:30 p.m. LIMELIGHT meet and greet. About two hundred fans take pics with us in front of our step and repeat, while Bam Bam keeps it moving with his favorite megaphone. We hug each and every one of you. Daniel may even lift you off the ground in a bear hug because he is very strong and mighty. We try to make every shot different. Jack balances a Red Bull on his head. Jonah kisses a fan on the forehead and tells her he likes her shirt. Corbyn accidentally gets poked in the eye but isn't mad about it. The step and repeat falls on our heads. We thank all the moms and dads who come through with handshakes and hugs, because they deserve love, too.

Btw, we are experts on hugs. Our next book should be called *The Art of Awkward Hugging* because we hug people at least four hundred times a day. **Here are five solid hugging tips:**

1. Don't be greedy. One hug!

2. Don't try to squeeze us to death like a boa constrictor. Remember, we need our lungs working properly to sing for you later.

3. Don't be mean. Telling Zach "You're annoying" is not flirting, even if it may be true.

4. Don't be smelly. Proper hygiene is greatly appreciated.

5. Don't be shy! Embrace the embrace! We really do love hugging you.

5:30–6:30 p.m. One hour of private time on the bus to gear up mentally for the show. We are not to be disturbed for any reason. If anyone bothers us, we sick Bam Bam on them! FYI, Zach usually takes a nap.

6:30 p.m. Refreshed, Zach heads over to the fence to sign autographs for the crowd, which is even bigger than before.

6:30:01 p.m. Security (and Jack) warns Zach not to go over to the fence because it will cause pandemonium.

6:30:02 p.m. Zach walks over to the fence anyway and it causes pandemonium.

6:30:03 p.m. Jack says, "Why doesn't he listen to me?"

6:32 p.m. We eat dinner from craft services and hang out in the parking lot with all of our close friends and family who've come to the show. It's like a giant picnic and for a minute we forget there's a show happening because everyone is having so much fun.

7:00 p.m. Time to get dressed and ready for the show! If our stylist, Teresita, isn't on the road with us, Stacy helps Jack and Zach, Jon helps Corbyn, and Reed helps Jonah pick out our clothes so we are color-coordinated. In the first part of the show, we all wear black, the second part we don our tuxes, and our third costume change is always something fun and unique that best represents our individual styles.

7:30 p.m. Our opener, Eben, hits the stage and KILLS IT.

8:14 p.m. Right before we go onstage, we huddle together and pray and thank God for where we are today. Then we do our secret handshake with all five of us guys. We don't go on stage if we haven't done this. There have been times the music started playing and we hadn't done it, so we did it really fast and then ran on stage!

Fun fact: The handshake was adapted from a handshake Daniel did back home with his friends. He randomly brought it to us, and we were like, This is dope. So now it's our band handshake!

Here's how to do it:

HANDSHAKE PHOTO DEMONSTRATION

Step 1:
Bro-hand hug

Step 2:
Index finger lock

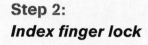

Step 3:
Thumb war grip

Step 4:
Sideways fist bump

Step 5:
High five

Step 6:
Snap

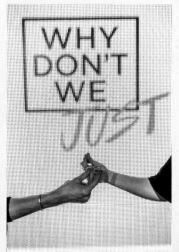

8:15 p.m. SHOWTIME. You sing every word to every song and we soak it in like oxygen. It lifts us up and gives us life.

9:30 p.m. Show's over! We take our final bows and run offstage. Daniel takes off his stage clothes and runs around backstage in his skivvies. "Naked guy coming through!" he shouts. We're all hyped up on adrenaline and high on life. This is what it's all about for us. We feel blessed to be doing what we love.

10:00 p.m. VIP OVERTIME. The same fans who met us first get an intimate private after party with us to talk about the show and say goodbye. We give out many more hugs and take more selfies, even though now we're the ones who smell! But nobody cares because all of us are so amped up and happy to be alive. When it's time to go, it's possible there will be some sobbing (and it's not Jonah).

10:30 p.m. We pile back on the bus and head to our next stop on the tour. Rinse and repeat every day...for the next year!

What It's Like on the Bus

There's no other way to put it: Our bus is DOPE. It's called the Stallion and it's huge. It has eight private bunks—five for us, one for our road manager, Bam Bam, one for our photographer, Zach Caspary, and one for Eben. It has two flat-screen TVs, a mini kitchen (none of us cook), and a bathroom with a shower (but none of us really use it unless we have to). Also, we have guitars stacked in the shower and we're too lazy to move them. The sign on the bathroom door says "No Farting Zone," which seems counterproductive but is very necessary because Zach farts a lot.

We always have hotel rooms booked in each city, two guys per room, and that's where we get ready for shows. In case you're wondering, we haven't trashed a hotel room . . . yet! We don't usually even sleep in the rooms because we're usually on our way to the next stop on the tour. Plus, it's way more fun to sleep on the bus and hang out with the guys all night. We have a lounge set up with an Xbox and also a mini recording studio, so when the mood strikes, and it strikes a lot, we can write songs and make demos together. The sound system is SICK. It will blow your head off!

We have so many feels about our tour bus:

Corbyn: I like the feel of it; it's like teleporting. You get on the bus, reminisce about the crazy moments of the show, break off to your bunk, fall asleep, and when you wake up in the morning, the sun is shining and you're in Louisville, Kentucky! You're like, NO WAY, how did I get here?

Daniel: The bus is like heaven. I'd rather have a ten-hour bus ride than a half-hour flight. The bunk rocks you to sleep. One time we filled the whole bus up to the ceiling with balloons, even the bathroom. You opened the door and it was like, WHOOSH! It was fun until we had to clean it up.

Jonah: We stopped at Walmart once and Jack came out with a giant panda mask. He got back on the bus and turned on Usher's "OMG" and was dancing like crazy with these moves that were so bad they were good. He danced for an hour straight.

Jack: The hairspray sometimes gets a little out of control because we're in an enclosed space. But, like, Corbyn insists his hair has got to be up. He'll be like, "Really sorry, Earth, but the hair's gotta have its moment."

Zach: One thing I don't like about tour is living out of a ton of suitcases. But I figured out how to do it right on the bus. I have one suitcase and it's super organized—the top has my underwear and socks, a little lower you have pants and shirts, then on top my jackets. I have one separate duffel bag for all my shoes.

Where You'll Find Us in Our Rare Downtime

Shopping

Zach is a shopaholic! He loves browsing for vintage stuff on Melrose in LA, 3rd Street Promenade in Santa Monica, and, most of all in New York City. But we're always like, "You can't just wander off, bro!"

Skateboarding

Once, in the middle of Nebraska, we rode our skateboards down a big hill in a little college town. Sometimes it's nice to get away from the craziness of the big cities.

Sightseeing

We rarely have time off to explore but when we went to Europe for two weeks—visiting amazing cities like Paris, Helsinki, Amsterdam—we had two days to be tourists. In London, we went to that giant Ferris wheel called the Eye and also Buckingham Palace. But one of us who shall remain nameless (cough, Zach, cough) posted it on Snapchat and all of a sudden thirty girls full-on sprinted across Hyde Park toward us and we had to run away. So we never got to meet Will and Kate and Harry and da Queen.

One thing we did that was super cool was a guided Beatles tour in Hamburg, Germany, which Paul McCartney once called "the naughtiest city in the

world." The Beatles played there a lot before they got really big, so we saw the infamous Star-Club and an alleyway where John Lennon puked once. We are all huge Beatles fans and it really motivated us (not the puking).

Eating

We're always on the hunt for Jimmy John's, Chipotle, and pizza! There's a little dive next to our hotel in New York City called Fluffy's. It's open twenty-four hours, so we all sneak out in the middle of the night for a slice.

The Beach

If there's a body of water with sand in your city, we will find it and chillax on it.

Where We Can't Wait to Go Next

Corbyn: Milan, Italy, because it's the fashion capital of the world. My favorite food is Italian and my girlfriend is Italian. Italy just seems like IT for me!

Daniel: Greece! I want to stay in one of those beautiful white houses on the Mediterranean Sea.

Jack: I want to skydive in Dubai! This guy Jay Alvarrez makes really artsy videos of him loving life and nature. He went skydiving in Dubai and it was so cool. I'm a very creative, artsy kind of guy, too. I want to free-fall in the air and look at that beautiful sight.

Jonah: Bora Bora! I want to sleep in one of those huts on stilts out in the middle of the water.

Zach: I want to go shopping in Hong Kong!

CHAPTER 13

The Best Night of Our Lives

Asking us which show was our favorite is like asking your mom which child she loves most. We have to say we love them all equally buuuuuuuuuuuttttttttttttttt one secretly holds a special place in our hearts! On December 9, 2017, Why Don't We played our first arena show, Z100's Jingle Ball at...drumroll please... Madison Square Garden in New York City.

Our first time playing the Garden was unforgettable. First of all, Zach, at sixteen, was the second-youngest person to ever perform at a sold-out show at the iconic stadium (Justin Bieber was the youngest, at fifteen). Just two years earlier, Zach had busked outside of Jingle Ball in Dallas. So it was quite emotional. Beyond that amazing milestone, we kicked off the Ball, opening for acts like the Chainsmokers, G-Eazy, Sam Smith, Demi Lovato, Charlie Puth, Halsey (she was super sweet to us!), and the headliners . . . Taylor Swift and Ed Sheeran! We were going to be sharing a stage with our idol!

The show had the biggest names in pop, and we were the underdogs. When we stepped on stage, our hearts beating a million miles per second, it was pitch black. Then they lit up our silhouettes and we saw 20,000 people just losing

their minds. We could have sung forever but were only allowed a quick, ten-minute set of five songs—"Air of the Night," "Nobody Gotta Know," "Something Different," "Help Me Help You," and "These Girls." New York crowds are tough—they've seen it all—so we were blown away when they not only liked us, but knew our songs and sang along. We walked off stage going, "What just happened?" We still have chill bumps to this day.

It was so surreal to have a whole arena scream for you, it was such an adrenaline rush. But then the night got even more cuckoo for Cocoa Puffs in the good way. We were so hyped up already, when suddenly our managers told us we were invited into Taylor Swift's greenroom! Wait, what? Alrighty, then! She'd already left us some signed merch, with a note that said, "Hey guys, congrats on your successful year! Much more to come. Keep killing it!" We thought that was so nice. But now the queen of pop had summoned us into her chamber! We gotta tell the rest of it in first person.

Corbyn: I splashed a little YSL cologne on. I wasn't tryna pick Taylor up, I was trying to come across as a mature young man. When we walked in there, her greenroom smelled like the most beautiful botanical garden. It was a royal scent. I thought, "What new land am I in?" Our greenroom smelled like carrots, ranch dressing, and hairspray.

Zach: It smelled amazing in there.

Jack: So we walk in and Taylor's sitting there with Ed Sheeran, like right there. They're like, "Hey, what's up!"

Jonah: Ed was like, "Why Don't We!" He knew us.

Corbyn: I looked to the right and Ed Sheeran was just chilling on the couch. I went over and shook his hand and we talked about their first arena shows. He asked how it was to be in our first Garden show and they were super stoked for us and super happy.

Daniel: Taylor asked us about our first MSG show and told us about hers and

opening for Rascal Flatts. She was always asking us questions. We were like, "Oh, but how was yours?" And she was like, "No, I want to know how you guys are doing!"

Jack: She is really tall. She was taller than me. I got to stand next to her in a picture.

Corbyn: Taylor was so sweet.

Jonah: Same with Ed. He was so curious about *you*. He really listened, like to get to know the other person. Nowadays, I'm sure everyone's trying to pull him in every direction and get a little bit of his time. To see someone at that level still be that grounded, right in the moment, and be able to have a convo was cool.

Zach: There were two of the craziest stars in the world, right in front of us. And I think Jack Antonoff and, like, Channing Tatum or somebody was in the back.

Jonah: It was Ryan Reynolds.

Daniel: Ryan Gosling walked around the corner and said, "Hey man, I'm Ryan." I was like, "I know! What!" Like I wouldn't know who he was! It was nuts!

Jonah: It was Ryan Reynolds.

Corbyn: I was told Ryan Gosling was in the room. I don't remember meeting him, I think because I was in such a mental frenzy.

Jack: Ed said, "Congratulations, you guys are killing it. You guys are going to blow up."

Corbyn: They loved our music and this was when we were in the works with Ed on "Trust Fund Baby," so it was cool to meet him after we cut it. He told us he loved the song and loved our vocals. Yay!

Daniel: Ed was like, "Yo, I love y'all's vibe and music, man." And I was like, "You, too, man! I have for a while actually!"

Jonah: He said he was looking forward to seeing what we do. To come from him, that was HUGE.

Zach: The second song I ever learned on guitar was Ed's "Thinking Out Loud." Taylor was so nice. They're actually dope people. You never know how stars are going to act, but they're just people.

Daniel: The reason why they're so successful is because they have the talent of a diva, but they also have the realness of any other person.

Jack: It was just so dope to see our idols say you're going to be us, basically. When we left, we were like, "Wow, that was legendary!"

Corbyn: When we got out of there, I was like, "Wait, Ryan Gosling was in the room?"

Jonah: It was Ryan Reynolds.

FAMILY BONDING AT THE BALL

One of the other incredible things about that night was that our families came to NYC and met each other for the first time. All of our moms, dads, brothers, and sisters flew out for the show and formed a lifelong bond. Ever since, they've been their own kind of family. The most exciting thing of all is that three of our families (Seaveys, Herrons, and Averys) have moved to the same apartment complex near the beach in LA. Jonah's and Corbyn's families are planning on moving there, too! On our last tour stop in LA, we all hung out at the pool and barbecued and played Ping-Pong. It was so much fun.

Our moms also have a group chat and they text each other any time something exciting happens, which is almost all the time. The bond between our families is for life.

Carrie Frantzich: When Why Don't We comes through Minnesota on tour, we host at our home so they enjoy a home-cooked meal and some downtime. I'm so happy for Jonah that he is connected with these other fine young men. They have become interconnected like family. The other Why Don't We families are becoming our extended family as well.

Kristin Stanford: When the boys had their very first show in New York, all of the families stayed in the same hotel. We all went to dinner at a Japanese steakhouse

and had a blast—veggies, steak, shrimp, and sake flying through the air and into our mouths. All of the siblings get along, too! There are so many talented kids—some of the sisters joke about forming a singing group called "Why Don't She."

Myta Herron: I love those girls so much! We are all super close. We are also a major support system for each other, that's for sure! Because it's not always easy. We know we can lean on each other. We all have relatively big families and our kids are all around the same ages, so it's super fun when we do get to hang out together.

Keri Seavey: Some of my favorite memories with the other moms are dancing and screaming like teenagers at the boys' concerts! We all have a common bond in wanting the holistic best for our boys and that is what initially caused such a strong connection between us. We always joked about buying a very large Why Don't We vacation home, so now that it's becoming a reality, Carrie Frantzich can cook for us all the time!

Saskia Vol: I can't wait to live closer to each other. We often joked about all living in one huge compound together and now we're actually doing it!

CHAPTER 14

We + You

**"Y'all go so hard for us 24/7.
You guys are the best."
—Corbyn**

Hands down, the best part about touring is finally getting to meet THE LIMELIGHTS! Yasss, kweens, that means YOU. At first, we weren't sure our solo followers would like the idea of us all being in one big band and merging fan groups. But the Why Don't We family came together in a heartbeat. It felt right from the get-go, there was so much love and excitement. THE LIMELIGHTS are the most amazing fans to us—and each other. You meet online and one of you is from Florida and another from California, and you fly across the country to hang out!

It's crazy to see all these friendships form through us. A big movement is happening and it's so incredible to watch through our eyes. At our shows, we see fans run up to each other and cry and hug and we're like, "What the heck?" It's all of you talking over social media for so long and finally meeting up. It's awesome. We always want to keep that going—appreciating our music and connecting with cool people through it.

Btw, we absolutely love meeting our fans. We love the hype when we show up to the venue, get off the bus, and girls are screaming. You're so happy to see us and hear our voices. It's so fun that we made an impact like that. It will never get old.

Meet and Greets

We never want to be the kind of artists who are kept behind glass like zoo animals or a boring museum exhibit. All of us have a blast seeing you at our meet and greets (though Jack gets a teeny bit of anxiety, so go easy on him!). It's rad when we recognize you from social media. It's getting a little harder now because there are more and more fans every day, but we still definitely put together faces with usernames. Please don't be offended that we won't know your real names. It's so much easier to remember something unique like mcmuffinz4ever or cutiebesson than Kate. There are 5,432 Kates!

We appreciate each and every one of you, especially all the girls who are obsessed with Corbyn but respect that he has a girlfriend. It's okay to get a hug and tell him, "Omg, you are like the perfect boyfriend!" or "You are the boyfriend I wish I had!" Es no muy bueno to try to make out with him. Which nobody has done yet, thankfully!

You're all so considerate—and generous! We tweet a lot about our favorite foods and you bring it on every night! Sometimes we are diabolical and tweet certain things on purpose, knowing we'll get them. One time, Daniel tweeted he liked watermelon, Jonah peanuts, Jack Gushers, Zach Oreos, and Corbyn

Nutter Butters. The next show we got fifty watermelons and three hundred of the other snacks! We took it on the bus in giant trash bags and the indescribable amount of treats filled up the entire bottom bunk area. The watermelon smelled so bad, we didn't know what to do with them.

One time Daniel wrote that he loved Sour Patch Kids and he got five hundred bags in one night. He ate so many of them, he was sure he gained thirty pounds overnight. We hate the idea of throwing perfectly good food out, so now, after every show, what we can't eat gets taken to the local fire department. P.S. Corbyn no longer loves Nutter Butters. If he sees them, he gets nauseous. Please do not bring those ever again. The Nutter Butter saga must end.

A lot of you also bring us gift cards from Starbucks and Chipotle. After spending your hard-earned cash on tickets to the show, we don't want you to spend more money on us! But just so you know, we love gift cards. When we wake up in the morning, we get coffee using them and it's the sweetest thing. Or we'll pull up in a new city and we got Chipotle cards in our wallets and we're all, "Let's go!"

How You Can Catch Our Eye Onstage

If you can't make it to a meet and greet, it's still possible to have a karmic connection with one of us during the show! Here are the best ways to grab our attention from the audience. We see you, too, nosebleeders!

Corbyn: It's really cool when fans just go hard. They're not only there to be at the concert—they're there to be in the music and be in the moment and let loose and have a great time. So when I see a hand fly in the air, I'm like, "AH YES! You're going all out! Go you!" Just try not to faint. Zach stopped the show once to help a girl who passed out.

Jack: To get my attention, hold up a poster that says, "I love your noodles,

Jack!" I like when fans write or shout out an inside joke I've said before or tweeted. Like, if I'm on stage and a girl screams, "YO, I HAVE YOUR GUSHERS!" I pay attention.

Jonah: One specific show there was a girl in the front row and we kept looking at each other. The whole time I kept going back to her. It was real. It happens. I'd say just be into it. Be in the moment instead of making a video or texting friends. I know you want to document it for later, but just be there!

Zach: Bring a really amazing sign! Like, "Zach is my boyfriend" or "Will you marry me, Zach?" If you can make me laugh during the show, I'll look at you and say, "Yes, yes, yes!" and we'll all freak out together. It's so fun making someone's day.

How Do You Always Find Us?

When not performing, we're not hanging upside down like bats in a cave waiting for the next show. We're human beings, who go out and about in the world, and it is very possible to cross paths with us. And you do. Somehow, no matter where we are and how careful we are not to post things that will pinpoint our location, you find us. One time, we were on the eighth floor of a hotel and we looked out the window and fifty of you were looking directly at us. Okay,

fine, you found the hotel, but how did you know what room we were in?!

You're like Rizzoli and Isles, expert detectives, and we kind of dig it. We just ask, if at all possible, that you please approach us less like a swarm of bees and more like a wild tiger in the jungle . . . with care and caution!

We've had some hilarious, slightly terrifying situations being chased by fans. On our first radio promo tour, we had to make a mad dash to our bus because five hundred girls tried to tackle us, yank Jack's hair out, and rip off our shirts to see our studly, hairless chests. Zach went the wrong way (it might have been on purpose, jury is still out on that one) and was surrounded by a group of wild-eyed ladies who grabbed his clothes and unintentionally scratched his face. After he finally clawed his way back on the bus, we drove away with a gaggle of girls pounding the windows. They almost got run over!

Another time, in Milwaukee, we were sleeping on the bus parked outside our hotel when around 3:00 a.m. we heard someone blasting "Something Different" outside. It was loud, then soft, then stopped, then got loud again, then stopped. We peeked out the window and saw five carfuls of fans circling the bus! We went outside to say hi, which was a huge mistake, because they came running and chased us right back into the bus. Hey, you drove all this way and we could have had a nice convo! The next morning we went outside and they left us cookies with a note saying, "Sorry for keeping you up all night!"

The thing is, if you're calm, we will hang with you. We are with the same (mostly male) road crew 24/7, so we want to meet new people! On tour in San Francisco, it was pouring rain and we saw a bunch of dedicated fans standing outside our bus for hours before our show getting soaked. We felt really bad, so we convinced our tour manager, Bam Bam, to open the emergency hatch on the roof of the bus. We climbed up there and did an acoustic version of "Trust Fund Baby" and everyone was so

happy, it didn't matter that we all looked like drowned rats!

Another time Daniel was at Disneyland with his brother and sister. Someone posted a Snap of him, and within minutes, local girls with yearly Disney passes found him at the park. One bold seventeen-year-old asked if he'd go on a ride with her, and he said, "Sure, why not!" They stood in line together and she told him every funny fact she knew about Disneyland.

Don't You Know Who We Are?

Getting recognized is still surreal. We're not really mainstream yet, but we're like when your mom gets a new car and then you see that car everywhere. Corbyn was thrilled to be recognized by the cashier at Taco Bell. "You're that guy!" she said. Close enough!

One time we were at a Red Robin in San Antonio, Texas, after a radio show. We made the mistake of driving our bus to the restaurant and we really made the mistake of posting a photo of a red balloon. Everyone knows the red balloon is at Red Robin. Next thing we know, the place filled up like a concert venue. It was nuts. The owner was like, "What is going on?" We snuck out through the kitchen and all the cooks and waitstaff clapped and saluted us.

I guess one downside to all of this would be not being able to go anywhere. That would suck. If it ever gets to that point, we're going to "crap our pants," as Zach says so elegantly. And just wear a hat and sunglasses! We can deal with it.

You Matter to Us

Our fans have a special place in our hearts. Like, for Jack, you guys are the ones who made him feel good about how he dressed. You had no problem with how he looked; you loved it. And he'll never forget that.

We like having feedback from and direct contact with you and that's why we leave our DMs open. We can't get to everyone but we try to have normal conversations with as many of you as possible. Don't be surprised to hear from Jonah if you're going through a tough time. He reaches out to fans all the time to spread messages of love and positivity.

Because of social media, we really are something different than bands from the past. We appreciate the personal connection we have with our fans and will never take that for granted. It's how we started out, it's how we made it to the top, and it's how we'll have careers that last a lifetime. So, if you do see us in person, don't be afraid to give us a hug. You've put so much effort into us and we want to thank you for that. We feel like the luckiest guys alive every day. We're living our dreams because of YOU.

We need you in our life like LIMELIGHT!

DANIEL'S BIGGEST FAN

On our Something Different tour, at the end of one of our shows, I saw Harry Connick, Jr. in the crowd bobbing his head. I didn't even know he was coming. I came out after to see him in his truck and he said, "Hey, man, I'm really proud of you. Keep doing it."

PART III

IN THIS
TOGETHER

CHAPTER 15

Cuz I'm Really, Really into You

Do you have a picture of Jack hanging in your locker? Write "Mrs. Daniel Seavey" in your notebook with a heart over the "i"? Carve Corbyn's name into your desk at school? Stan and plan your wedding to Zach? Make out with your pillow and pretend it's Jonah's pillowy lips?

You don't have to daydream about what it would be like to date us anymore, because we're going to tell you exactly how it is—heaven! JK. You can decide for yourself if we're boyfriend material! (Corbyn is exempt because, as of writing this book, he's the only one of us with a real girlfriend).

Jack

My type: I love personalities. If she happens to be good looking that's a bonus. I love a girl with a nice smile, who doesn't care what people think. Who is very happy with herself and with life. That's all you need you know.

My bf personality: I'm kinda romantic. I'm a silly, funny, goofy goober. In public, I'll do stupid things to embarrass my girlfriend, like yell an inappropriate word really loudly.

My worst breakup: I recently went through it after nine months with someone. I knew I needed to focus on music and it would be hard to make her as happy as I wanted to, so I ended things. I said, "I'm sorry. I know this is for the better." She was very sweet and we were really into each other. It just wasn't the right time.

Would you use a dating app?: I have before but then I said, "This isn't a good idea!" I want to meet her in person. I feel like meeting on an app makes the story less exciting and romantic. If you met them in person, you could say, "Man, I really loved her smile." You can't say that through the phone.

Most romantic move: My ex loved Disneyland, so I got her a bracelet, earrings, and a necklace with Mickey Mouse on it. I had them all wrapped up and we went out for a nice dinner and a movie. It was a cute date.

Jonah

My type: Someone I can have a good convo with. I'm kinda into tomboys, someone who has a little grit. Not crazy about a lot of makeup. I'll meet a beautiful girl, and suddenly I'm not into her anymore because we can't connect. It's all about chemistry.

My bf personality: I can get too focused on my girl. Like, just talk to her all the time and not hang with my other friends. That's not healthy.

My worst breakup: When I was sixteen, I had a girlfriend who was nineteen and that was not a good situation. She was super controlling. I had to go to Florida for a show and she flew down because she said she didn't trust me with other girls there. What's more important than trust? It taught me a lot. I haven't had a girlfriend in three years!

Best breakup music: John Mayer

Bad boi behavior: I went to Knott's Berry Farm with two girls but didn't realize both thought I was on a date with them. I was holding both of their hands, skipping around clueless, and they got mad at me.

Most romantic move: One Valentine's Day, I wrote a poem for a girl in cursive.

Biggest turnoff: Being cocky and bragging

Dream girl: I just want to be in a relationship where we're each other's best friends.

Dream wedding: I want to get married but I don't want the whole big thing. My parents eloped to Vegas and that was kind of cool.

Daniel

My type: A girl I've been friends with first. If you're really close friends, there's so much more depth to your relationship. It shows a lot about them if they can just be a friend first.

Turnoff: No sense of humor! Cockiness!

My bf personality: I think I'm giving and caring. I want to make sure my girl is happy and comfortable at all times.

Would you date a fan?: If she was cool!

Best breakup music: Anything by Adele

Most romantic move: In seventh grade, I had a huge crush on a girl. I was afraid to tell my parents because I didn't even know if I was allowed to date. On Valentine's Day, I scraped up enough money to get her a teddy bear, chocolates, and roses and set it all up in a classroom at school as a surprise for her.

Dream wedding: On a peaceful beach with special sand that doesn't get in your shoes.

Zach

My type: We can laugh at the stupidest stuff together. I really like independent girls, who know who they are. And can make me happy and change my world.

Biggest turnoff: Smells bad!

First kiss: In fourth grade, I was outside on the playground next to a pillar. One girl was a lookout while I kissed another girl behind the pillar!

My bf personality: I think I'm a sweet boyfriend: I decorated one girl's bedroom for homecoming! And I'm very understanding. I'm good with advice. Like, if you need help, I'm always here.

My worst breakup: There have been a couple times when I extended things for like two months just because I felt bad. I was their world and I didn't want to hurt them. I loved them enough for that but I didn't really feel the relationship as much. I had to find ways to ease out of it.

Most romantic move: In middle school, I liked a girl but I couldn't get her.

So I wrote a song about the struggle and then the next year, I got the girl! But I never told her about the song. I've never performed for a girl. I couldn't do it back then. Too shy. Now I probably could!

Have you ever been in love?: I'm deeply in love with my bed.

CORBYN + CHRISTINA

Corbyn has been dating New York City beauty blogger Christina Marie Harris, aka @beautychickee, for two years, mostly long-distance because of their busy schedules. The two are so adorable and there for each other. Christina has gone on tour with the guys, and Corbyn has famously let her give him a makeover on her vlog. He looked v. pretty!

WHO WAS YOUR FIRST GIRLFRIEND?

Christina! Freshman year I had some of the popular girls on me, but I didn't realize it because I wasn't good with girls. I'd be at a football game and my friend would say, "Kayla wanted me to tell you you're hot." And I was like, "Okay, thanks." I'm STILL not good with girls. I just got lucky!

HOW DID YOU MEET CHRISTINA?

Through the internet. So millennial! She told me she had a thing for me. I didn't believe her and she was like, "Didn't you get my hints?" I was fifteen at the time and had never even held a hand or had a kiss. I didn't know!

WHAT DO YOU LOVE MOST ABOUT HER?

She has the biggest personality. She's funny and really loud and Italian so her whole family is so loud and funny. She's very independent, she's organized, she's a businesswoman.

WAS IT LOVE AT FIRST SIGHT THE FIRST TIME YOU MET?

There was this big social media event at Universal Studios in Orlando and I convinced my mom to let me go alone to meet her. Thanks again, Mom! I was getting butter beer and Christina ran up to me from behind and I was like, "YES!" We went on all the Harry Potter rides together.

DID YOU MAKE THE FIRST MOVE?

We were sitting on a bench after a ride and I so badly wanted to wrap my arms around this girl. But I couldn't do it. I thought I'd creep her out. Then we got up and I put my arm around her. It was a big step for me.

WHAT WAS YOUR MOST FUN DATE SO FAR?

She asked me to her prom on Long Island. I stayed at her house for a few days—separate rooms, of course!

HOW DO YOU MANAGE LONG-DISTANCE?

It's cool. We get to live our own separate worlds and then we converge at the end of the day and it's just perfect. She really likes to talk, so on FaceTime I can just let her talk the whole time and I play videos in the background and listen halfway. It's gotten to the point where we can be silent for like three hours and we're fine.

WHY DO YOU THINK IT'S LASTED SO LONG?

We're very laid-back and we have a lot of trust in each other. Trust and communication—everyone says those are the most important thing and they're not lying.

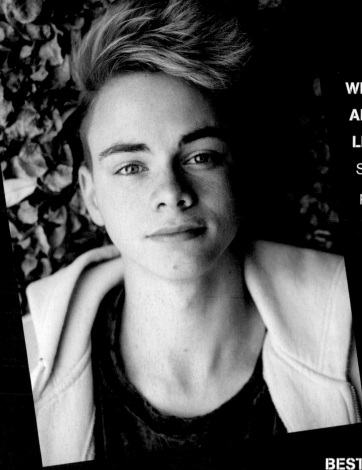

WHAT DOES SHE THINK ABOUT ALL OF YOUR LIMELIGHT LOVE?

Sometimes fans will go on her page and leave comments like, "Corbyn doesn't love you. You don't deserve him." She doesn't get jealous because she knows my intentions. It helps because she comes from the same world. She has her fans so she knows, fans are fans. Personal life is personal life.

BEST RELATIONSHIP ADVICE?

If you let stuff fester and boil, it will come out like a storm. So you can have either one giant storm that can potentially cause millions of dollars in damage, like a hurricane, or you can have a bunch of little showers. There's always sunshine after the rain.

HOW DO THE OTHER GUYS FEEL ABOUT HER?

They love her! Whenever she comes over she makes us home-cooked meals. We have pasta night, with chicken cutlets and Caesar salad. It's usually just dudes all the time. It's nice to have a woman around!

CHAPTER 16

5/5 = 1

"We're the five best friends that anyone could have. . . ."
—Jack, singing like Zach Galifianakis in *The Hangover*

We've been through hard times together to get to where we are now. Through good times and bad, we learned to lean on each other, look out for each other, keep each other in check and, most important, give each other advice on girls!

Our handshake may seem silly but it's everything to us. We do it after tough breaks and amazing achievements. Sad moments and deep talks. That hand-shake is the solidifier of our brotherhood. We're brothers for life.

Yes, we are individuals but also one-fifth of something that is bigger than our-selves. We have a special connection because we're in a band together. None of us ever thought we'd be in a band like this. We always looked up to bands like One Direction. What guy hasn't thought, "Yo, it must be cool to be in a band of five guys and all these girls love you." You look at them and freak out. But how impossible would it be to find four guys who are not only on the same page musically but have the same dedication and work ethic? It's one in a billion.

"I've grown up a lot."
–Zach

It's crazy that this band happened. It just fell into place and now we get to share this out-of-body experience together. We can't imagine doing this solo and how lonely that would be. We need each other. If any of us gets off track or starts getting cocky and not humble, we're like, "YO, quit doing that. Stand back." If someone starts to slip, we get on 'em. It's because we genuinely care.

Our friendship outside of music is solid. We spend every waking minute together but we still want to hang when we're supposed to be apart! Lately, in the morning, we all love to go to the gym together. On our rare off time, we always plan adventures together, like hiking in Joshua Tree or snowboarding in Aspen. When we say we do everything together, we mean it!

OUR HONORARY BROTHER BAM BAM

Early on, we had a show in Port-land, Daniel's hometown, and his older brother Tyler came and hung out. Our manager was like, "Hey, we could use an extra hand on the road, does Daniel's brother want to come with us?" That day he left with us and he's been with us ever since. He sleeps on our bus. He's our road manager but we all treat him like an older brother. So, if we're doing anything dumb, he's the first guy to tell you and set you straight. Tyler's hilarious, he walks like a penguin, always talks at volume 10 (20 with his beloved megaphone), and he's super strong. One time he slammed the van door really hard, and from that day forward, he was dubbed Bam Bam, like the kid from *The Flintstones*. It bugged Tyler so much, we tweeted out in all caps, "EVERYONE! TYLER'S NEW NICKNAME IS BAM BAM," and it just stuck. We even made him an official Instagram account called @BamBamontheGram. Tyler doesn't have access to the account, so we all run it. We post the most awful pictures of him possible and he only follows one person, Michelle Obama. He loves Michelle Obama—he just doesn't know it yet.

We give him a hard time because he's always waddling in and telling us what to do. But we love him and respect him. He's the one who makes sure we get out the door on time, have food for the day, and shoot our lines. It's not easy. His job is like herding cats!

In the Hizzy

To this day, it's never been hard living together. Last Christmas, we got three weeks off to go home, which was our longest vacation since we started this whole crazy journey. But by the end of three weeks, we were so ready to come back. That's because our new house is so DOPE.

Before we went on tour in March 2018, the five of us, plus Bam Bam, lived in a cool Airbnb in the Hollywood Hills, which put us close to all the action. Within minutes, we could skateboard over David Bowie's or the Beatles' star on the Hollywood Walk of Fame. So many famous artists lived in our neighborhood, and the aura inspired us.

Our house, which we gave up when we went on tour, so now we're technically homeless, was always filled with music, laughter, weird smells wafting from the kitchen, and the glorious sound of Ping-Pong balls ricocheting off the walls. When you walked in, the first thing you'd see, of course, was the Ping-Pong table in the dining room. We took the dining table out because it's not like we had that many formal meals. None of us cooked, unless Corbyn's girlfriend came to visit. We pretty much lived on Postmates delivery, Uncrustables, frozen pizza, Bagel Bites, and taquitos.

You can only imagine what a biohazard the place *could* have been with five guys living there. Luckily, we had a little robot named Alfred that mopped the floors. Jack and Daniel are the neatest, and Corbyn can be when he wants to be (just don't look in his closet). Jack and Daniel have been known to slam a ton of caffeine and go on cleaning frenzies that got the whole house sparkling in like ten minutes. Everything just disappeared right before your eyes. It was supernatural.

Corbyn, Jack, Jonah, and Zach had bedrooms upstairs. Corbyn's room had access to the roof, so if we couldn't find him, he was probably out there stargazing and contemplating the fate of the universe. Down below was an apartment for Bam Bam and Daniel, who had a little recording studio with a monitor and speakers set up in his room.

Zach, shocking, was the house prankster. Once, he kept going into Jack's and Corbyn's room and taking one shoe at a time and putting them in his closet. They eventually ran out of shoes and were like, "Yo, who is taking all of our shoes?" Zach wouldn't fess up for a week. Then he stole their toothbrushes and headphones. After he finally admitted it, the next time Zach went out of town, they got sweet revenge. They took everything he owned and hid it in their rooms. It was hilarious.

"They are so revered by their fans but they're like five little brothers to me."
—band photographer/videographer Zack Caspary

"You can't be around these guys and have a negative thought. They are so supportive. They are like family."
—Eben, WDW's Invitation Tour opener

Most of the time, we are chill and get along like bruthas from another mutha. But with six guys under one roof, stuff can get gnarly if we're not in tune with each other. (Nice music pun!) We all tried to respect each other's privacy. Sure, we'd throw a good party here and there, but we didn't invite random people over constantly. Our motto was "MySpace is also YourSpace." So we had a bit of an approval process. Just ask and let's figure it out.

When we did have issues, we were open with each other about it. We had house/band meetings to resolve issues. If one of us just called someone out, it was gonna be a problem. But if we were like, "Hey, we should all talk. What should we all work on?" it was an open table. It was more of a "let's get back on track" than a "you suck" vibe. Daniel is a natural leader and does speak up. Corbyn is pretty mature and often the guy who breaks the peace. He likes to chime in and have his opinion be heard and valued.

We've been smart about how to have a good relationship with each other. We hash it out quick, nip it in the bud. We're not in this to break up one day and sell the dream we made with each other. We're in this to have fun and make good music.

KING PONG

Okay, there is one thing we fight about the most... Ping-Pong! We're the most competitive people ever. We are Ping-Pong enthusiasts. We used to play every night when we were in LA. We'd go home, goof off, play Ping-Pong, and sing.

Zach: We got really good. We go crazy.

Jonah: I think I'm the best. We always had a table at my house growing up. It gets competitive, though. Daniel can give me a run for my money.

Daniel: I can beat both Jonah and Jack. I was crushing it but then Jonah went home for a week and he got really good.

Jack: Jonah isn't the best in Ping-Pong—he's the best *spinner*. When he hits it, it goes crazy directions, and you're like, How does he do that? I don't think any of us are the best. Okay, fine, Jonah does beat us a lot.

Corbyn: We all love to play Ping-Pong. That's a given.

Jack: I'm the skateboard guru. I'm not being cocky but I am the best.

CHAPTER 17

Life Is a Gift

On October 1, 2017, at 10:05 p.m., we were in Las Vegas, watching Blue Man Group perform at the Luxor Resort & Casino, when a mass shooter opened fire on the crowd at Route 91 Harvest, an outdoor country music festival, from the thirty-second floor window of the hotel next to us, killing 58 people and injuring 851. We had originally planned to go to the earlier showing of Blue Man Group. If we had, we could have been walking the Strip when the tragedy went down.

We feel so fortunate that we were there for each other that night, and to even be here to be able to tell you this story. We were having such a blast watching the show, especially when one of the actors stood over Jack and pretended to sit down on his face. Just before it was supposed to end, the actors suddenly waved goodbye, walked offstage, and the lights came up. We sat there for an hour confused, thinking they were having technical difficulties, until a voice on the intercom announced that there was an active shooter nearby, we were to remain seated and they were closing the doors.

For the next ten hours, we were placed on lockdown. We sat in the theater, huddled together, getting updates from our frantic families and friends on our cell phones, which were running out of juice and had spotty reception. Jonah's parents aren't glued to their phones 24/7, so he couldn't reach them the longest and he was very stressed out. Our tour manager, Jon, texted us that the shooter was in the hotel right next to the Luxor, connected by a bridge. We read rumors on the internet that a bomb may have been planted at the Luxor. Jack saw a Snapchat post by Instagram star Dan Bilzerian running away from the country concert as bullets sprayed around him. And meanwhile, our manager, Randy, was on the phone all night trying to figure out how to get us out of there.

It was a terrifying night, especially because we weren't allowed to leave and didn't know if that meant the killer was in our building. They passed out bananas and blankets and we tried to sleep, resting our heads on each other's shoulders, but it was futile. It was hard not to think the worst, especially with the scary news we were able to get on our phones, but we didn't panic; we kept each other calm. We just figured out an escape plan if something awful happened and we had to run out of there.

Finally, at 5:00 a.m., they let us go. We didn't know yet that it was the deadliest mass shooting in American history. As we walked out of the hotel, we just felt something awful in our guts. It was a very eerie feeling. There were no people or cars, just police everywhere. Jonah looked up and saw the two broken windows where the shootings happened. Jon and Tyler, who had been frantic about his brother Daniel, ran up to us and wrapped us in big hugs, then got us out of there.

We were so tired and in shock. And beyond grateful to be alive. We weren't shot at but it was still a life-changing experience. You think you're invincible and nothing's going to happen to you but this was a major reality check. You realize how quickly something can happen out of nowhere. Count your blessings and tell your friends and family you love them right now, because you just never know what tomorrow will bring.

CHAPTER 18

Thankful

We feel like the luckiest guys in the world. Here are a few things we're particularly grateful for:

Corbyn: I'm Thankful I'm Happy

I'm most thankful for my easygoingness. There's so much sadness out there, especially on the internet and with young girls in general. I like doing good, and I like being happy. I'm a very stress-free kind of guy. I wasn't always that way. I used to get caught up in the little things. Now I just sweep them away. Will this matter in ten minutes? Tomorrow? Probably not. So why dwell on it? I don't remember what clicked but now I don't take life too seriously. If I like something, I'll wear it, I'll buy it, I'll eat it, I'll drink it. Life is so much better not caring about being cool. It's cool to be interested in something and go through with it! Accomplish something! I'm thankful that my mom taught me kindness, and my dad taught me hard work and perseverance. It's a good mix, and I'm thankful I get to show people that.

Zach: I'm Thankful I'm a Role Model

It feels great. It's a weird feeling, if a fan touches me it's like, "I'm touching him!" I'm just me! The fact that millions of people look up to us is crazy, that we can make an impact in their lives being who we are and expressing ourselves. We're changing people's lives, so we don't ever want to let them down.

Jonah: I'm Thankful I Get to Make Art

I'm thankful I see it actually affect people's lives. That really has had the biggest impact on me, like when a girl tells us in the meet and greet, "You guys got me through a hard time in my life," or "I was really depressed" or "My dad died." There are a lot of stories like that, where we've helped them. That means so much because I know how that feels. When my mom was sick, my favorite artists got me through it. It's come full circle. Now I can do that for other kids out there.

Daniel: I'm Thankful I Earned Success

When I was bullied in high school, kids would always say *American Idol* was handed to me. With this band, I've proven that I made something great happen with my own hands. I took initiative and I worked hard to earn it. I love doing things for myself and stuff that no one told me to do but did just because I wanted to do it. I've had a lot of help along the way from so many amazing people who lifted me up and I'm grateful for that, too.

Jack: I'm Thankful I Can Give Back to My Family

It's really gratifying making a living doing what I love. I like to share my good fortune. This past Christmas, I brought my little sister, Isla, and my mom to Disney World. I spent a lot of money, but it was worth it, because I'd rather spend money on memories and not things.

When Isla opened her gift, it said, "Merry Christmas, Mouseketeer! Your adventure begins December 25, 2017." She looked at me and goes, "Is that today?" I said, "Yep, we're going tonight." She put her head down and started bawling.

CHAPTER 19

Coming Up Next

We are so stoked that Why Don't We is kicking booty but that doesn't mean we just stop dreaming. All of us have set big personal goals, too!

Jack: I have my personal goals in my phone: Buy a big beautiful house for my family, make a million dollars or more, drink more water, finish the Harry Potter series, buy my dream car (an Audi R8), go to Hawaii, save and invest more money! I would love to act; if we all did a comedy together like the Beatles, that would be so cool. I would love to get into producing, I just started making my own beats. My goal is to be a millionaire not because I care about money, but I feel that being a millionaire shows you have successfully made it, and you can successfully buy whatever you want for your family and whatever you want for yourself. I feel like that's a really cool thing. Success is so cool. When you finally make it, you can take a deep breath, look back, and say, "Wow, my hard work really paid off. I did it!

Zach: In five years, I'll only be twenty-one. I'll probably just get a big house in LA and chill. My number-one thing will be making sure to help my family and get them a nice house out here, too. Maybe I'll be in movies—by then hopefully I'll be acting. That would be fun!

Corbyn: My biggest goal in life is to be somebody and make a difference—regardless of what it is. To do something that affects a lot of people in an amazing way or helps out in an amazing way, or I get recognized for some sort of achievement or break-through. I'd like to call myself a businessman. I want to launch my own clothing line one day.

I want it to be unique and the kind of looks and shapes that I like. I'd love to see people wear my designs and express themselves. When we tour now, I'm focusing on the culture of where we visit, and why and how people dress and live a certain way. Acting, modeling, photography, I want to do it all!

Daniel: I want to have my own label. I want to use my platform to help other artists. The year I went home after *American Idol*, more than anything, I wanted someone to notice and appreciate my music. I want to find that person who is going through the same thing and has talent. Let's make something together!

Jonah: All I hope is that I'm happy and that I'm still doing what I love to do.

CHAPTER 20

The Future

1. Do our first stadium tour. When that happens, we'll be really happy. We want to sell out Wembley Stadium—that's 76,000 people!

2. Have a number-one song.

3. Change the world for the better. We see young people like us being empowered on the news all the time. We have opinions, too, and they deserve to be valued. Our generation is the future—we want to be part of that positive change.

4. Be there for people to lean on and look to for light, no matter what's going on in the world.

5. Always keep each other humble and connected. Twenty years from now, we all want to be happy and still be best friends and a band of brothers.

BYE, FOR NOW!

We hope you enjoyed our book—we had a blast remembering the good times, telling the funniest stories, and picking out our favorite photos. We've loved sharing our journey so far with you, and if we didn't say it enough already, we are very thankful to our fans for making our dreams come true.

But now the show must go on! We are so excited about the future, we are freaking out. We have a new album coming out with Atlantic Records, more sick videos on the way, and a world tour that will last a year and take us to incredible new places like Japan and Australia!

Hey, it's gonna be crazy busy, but no matter what happens, always expect the best from us . . . that means great music, positive vibes, and, of course, perfectly coiffed hair!

Peace out, LIMELIGHTS!

Acknowledgments

Thank you to all our friends, family, and loved ones who supported us through everything—you know who you are. We love you.